BOOKS

"The chief beauty about time is that you cannot waste it in advance. The next year, the next day, the next hour are lying ready for you, as perfect, as unspoiled, as if you had never wasted or misapplied a single moment in all your life. You can turn over a new leaf every hour if you choose."

~Arnold Bennett

ALSO by S. R. Adams

Hope to a Friend: Sunrise – Encouragement to Overcome

In the Works

Hope to a Friend: Sunrise – Encouragement While Waiting

31 DAYS
WITH
SHAN
Turning over a new leaf

S. R. ADAMS

S. R. Adams Brand, LLC   Oceanside, California

Copyright © 2017 by Shanquia Adams
All rights reserved,
including the right of reproduction
in whole or in part in any form.

In accordance with the U.S. Copyright Act of 1976, the scanning, uploading, and electronic sharing of any part of this book without permission of the publisher is unlawful piracy and theft of the author's intellectual property. No part of this book may be reproduced by any mechanical, photographic, or electronic process, or in the form of phonographic recording; nor may it be restored in a retrieval system, transmitted, or otherwise be copied for private use – other than for "fair use" as brief quotations embodied in articles and reviews. If you would like to use material from the book (other than for review purposes), prior written permission must be obtained by contacting the publisher at: info@sradams.com.

This publication contains the opinions and ideas of its author. It is intended to provide helpful and informative material on the subjects addressed in the publication. Use of any information in this book is classified as self-help. It is sold with the understanding that the author and publisher are not engaged in rendering medical, health, or any other kind of personal professional services in the book. The reader should consult his or her medical, health, or other competent professional before adopting any of the suggestions in this book or drawing inferences from it. The author and publisher specifically disclaim all responsibility for any liability, loss, or risk, personal or otherwise. Therefore, no responsibility for loss caused to any individual or organization acting on or refraining from action as a result of the material in this publication, directly or indirectly, can be accepted by S. R. Adams Brand, LLC or the author.

MATERIAL YOU SEND TO S. R. ADAMS BRAND, LLC WILL NOT BE TREATED AS CONFIDENTIAL. Anything you submit to us will be considered free of obligations to you regardless of circumstance. We will not pay you for the use of any content that you submit - unless otherwise agreed upon in witting prior to submission. Under no circumstances will we pay you for the use of your ideas or submissions. By submitting any material to S. R. Adams Brand LLC you agree to these terms in addition to the above.

Edited by Jefferson from FirstEditing

Printed in the United States of America

S. R. Adams Brand, LLC
P.O. Box 2269
Oceanside CA, 92051

International Standard Book Number
13 Digit: 978-0-9977465-8-7   10 Digit: 0-9977465-8-0

First Edition: September 2017
10 9 8 7 6 5 4 3 2 1

Library of Congress control number: 2017912315

31 DAYS WITH SHAN – Turning over a new leaf /S. R. Adams

To find out more about the S. R. Adams brand visit:
www.sradams.com.
Here you can shop, sign up for events, view inspirational messages, and more.
Please contact us regarding special discounts for bulk purchases at info@sradams.com

Many Blessings...

May the light of Love be with you to guide
and comfort you on your journey.

I Love You!

"Change will not come if we wait for some other person or some other time. We are the ones we've been waiting for. We are the change that we seek."

~President Barack Obama

Contents

Introduction   *xiii*

Are You Ready?   17

DAY 1 Humble Yourself   31

DAY 2 Break the Habit   39

DAY 3 Don't Fight the End   47

DAY 4 Learn When to Stop   55

DAY 5 Can't Change Them   63

DAY 6 Don't Feel Bad   71

DAY 7 You Owe Yourself   79

DAY 8 You Don't Need Them To   87

DAY 9 Because You Can   95

DAY 10 Don't Cross Wires   103

DAY 11 Trash Is Treasure   111

DAY 12 This to Make That   119

DAY 13 Time to Upgrade   129

DAY 14 Take Responsibility   137

DAY 15 Be Honest with Self   149

DAY 16 *A Fresh Start*	*157*
DAY 17 *Get Power Back*	*165*
DAY 18 *Aware of Purpose*	*173*
DAY 19 *Learn from Nature*	*183*
DAY 20 *Invent the New You*	*193*
DAY 21 *Positive Change*	*201*
DAY 22 *Turn Dirt into Mud*	*209*
DAY 23 *Stand Up*	*217*
DAY 24 *Start Moving*	*225*
DAY 25 *Capable of Achieving*	*233*
DAY 26 *Wishing for It All*	*241*
DAY 27 *Faith vs Stupid*	*251*
DAY 28 *Open the Door*	*259*
DAY 29 *Compassion for Others*	*267*
DAY 30 *Journey to Destiny*	*275*
DAY 31 *Be Patient*	*283*

Is it time to turn over a new leaf? Why wait? Start turning now! Every day for the next 31 days, you'll have the opportunity to do just that. Complete the provided exercises and simply turn the page. Yes, turning over a new leaf is that simple. Feel better by seeking to find solutions to the problems in your life. No worries. You can start fresh each day! Develop, grow, and become whoever it is you're destined to become.

Create Your New Leaf

Congratulations! You have a fresh start! Keep track of the new you. Once you've defined your wants vs needs and have divided the two, commit to yourself to achieve your goals by using the commitment contracts provided at the end of each day.

Positive Practice

I want to change because:
_____
_____
_____

The first thing I'd like to change is:
_____
_____
_____

Why?
_____
_____
_____

When do you plan to start?
_____
_____
_____

Where will you start?
_____
_____
_____

How do you plan to do it?
_____
_____
_____

My friend,

You have something to offer to the world – you. Present yourself! Not the "you" others want to see – the YOU you're meant to be. It can be uncomfortable to hear the truth at times. Sometimes, it's painful to see the truth. However, if the truth did not exist, flies would rule.

We're not here to please people. This can never truly be done. The nature of man is never satisfied. We eat and drink only to hunger and thirst again. Set your priorities, line them up, and keep them straight.

You're your number one priority. Yes, you're your responsibility. All that other stuff can wait. You are not beneficial to anyone when you're not happy. Your negativity and bad energy will spread like a deadly disease. It will stunt growth!

You're not here to please; you're here to serve. In order to serve, there's going to be times you'll have to stand while others sit. My friend, be fit for duty mentally, emotionally, spiritually, and physically. Don't compromise your true self for anyone – or anything. I like that quote by Dr. Seuss that says, "Be who you are and say what you feel, because those who mind don't matter and those who matter don't mind."

I wrote *31 Days with Shan* to share beneficial ways of becoming the best you while living in a world full of ups and downs. My goal is to encourage, motivate, and inspire you on your journey to enlightenment.

It is my desire that this book will help you come full circle in life. When you begin your journey, spend each day thinking about how to better yourself. Commit to you! Remember, yesterday is gone, today is now, and tomorrow has yet to come. There's still time to get it right. There's still time to turn over a new leaf.

Self-betterment requires you spend time carefully considering where you are and strategically planning to get to where you want, or need, to be. No worries. You're equipped, enough, and deserving!

Become! Let this book help you make it easier for yourself. Take it from me. I've learned a lot of easy things the hard way. I'm no expert. I am not your guru. My life has been full of trial and error. Mostly error, but it's through error that we learn how to get it right.

So, please consider me your friend. If you have anything you'd like to share, feel free to write me. I'd love to hear from you! S. R. Adams, P.O. Box 2269, Oceanside, CA 92051. Or visit www.sradams.com.

Present the Best You

Many Blessings,

S. R. Adams

"Always be a first-rate version of yourself instead of a second-rate version of someone else."

~Judy Garland

Are You Ready?

Let's see! I've provided this readiness test to measure your motivation. Answer all the questions honestly and take your time. After the test is completed calculate your score and then read the interpretation of your number range.

Readiness Test

Answer the following questions by marking *Yes*, *No*, or *Undecided*.

1. I am ready to change no matter what other people may think.
   Yes ( )   No ( )   Undecided ( )

2. I am ready to do things differently than what I have done in the past.
   Yes ( )   No ( )   Undecided ( )

3. I am ready to get rid of thoughts about myself and others that are broken, lack purpose, and do not fit.
   Yes ( )   No ( )   Undecided ( )

4. I am ready to change regardless of what others may think or say to or about me.
   Yes ( )   No ( )   Undecided ( )

5. I am ready to make the change even if it may temporarily cause conflict.
   Yes ( )   No ( )   Undecided ( )

6. I am ready to block out anyone who does not respect or support my efforts.
   Yes ( )   No ( )   Undecided ( )

7. I am tired of being unhappy in life.
   Yes ( )   No ( )   Undecided ( )

8. I am willing to commit to myself.
    Yes ( )   No ( )   Undecided ( )

9. I admit that I have been unsuccessful in my past attempts to change because I was not ready to change.
    Yes ( )   No ( )   Undecided ( )

10. I am ready for things in my life to function and flow better.
    Yes ( )   No ( )   Undecided ( )

11. I am willing to do the work and follow the steps it takes to get my desired outcome.
    Yes ( )   No ( )   Undecided ( )

12. I am willing to read this book and honestly use the information and tools provided to change myself, my lifestyle, and my behavior.
    Yes ( )   No ( )   Undecided ( )

13. I am willing to ask for help when and where needed.
    Yes ( )   No ( )   Undecided ( )

14. I am willing to confront unhealthy habits that get in my way.
    Yes ( )   No ( )   Undecided ( )

15. I am willing to confront those who may try to sabotage my efforts.
    Yes ( )   No ( )   Undecided ( )

16. I am willing to relocate and change jobs and/or my associations if that's what it takes.
    Yes ( )   No ( )   Undecided ( )

17. I am willing, ready, and able to get it together.
    Yes ( )   No ( )   Undecided ( )

18. I am ready to get organized in my life and am no longer willing to waste time.
    Yes ( )   No ( )   Undecided ( )

19. For better health, I am willing to make me my top priority.
    Yes ( )   No ( )   Undecided ( )

20. I am willing to dedicate at least five to thirty minutes a day for myself and myself only to plan for self-betterment.
    Yes ( )   No ( )   Undecided ( )

21. I am willing to give myself positive self-affirmations.
    Yes ( )   No ( )   Undecided ( )

22. I am ready and willing to be honest with myself.
    Yes ( )   No ( )   Undecided ( )

23. I am ready and willing to stop lying to myself and others about why I can't seem to get or keep it together.
    Yes ( )   No ( )   Undecided ( )

24. I am ready and willing to take action in every area of my life.
    Yes ( )   No ( )   Undecided ( )

25. I am willing to admit that I have some problems, but I will not let these problems damage my commitment to myself.
    Yes ( )   No ( )   Undecided ( )

26. I admit that I must take responsibility for my life, and I am committed to making permanent changes.
    Yes ( )   No ( )   Undecided ( )

27. I am willing to say out loud that I am willing to change my lifestyle for less stress, better function, and overall well-being.
    Yes ( )   No ( )   Undecided ( )

28. I am ready to turn over a new leaf!
    Yes ( )   No ( )   Undecided ( )

Calculate your score

How many "yes" answers do you have? _____

Interpretation of the number

0 to 5: Content

If your score is low, I recommend you wait a few weeks and then take the test again. You're content with the way things are now and not ready to face issues or make changes where necessary. No one can make a change for you – you have to be willing to make a change for yourself. To be honest, until you're ready to put forth the effort it's going to take to make the necessary changes in your life, this book will do you no good. You currently enjoy being in your comfort zone and will avoid any level of change suggested.

If you're saying to yourself: "My life the way it is doesn't really bother me," "I can focus and function just fine the way things are," "My family and friends don't really mind my behavior," "My thoughts and dysfunction have no effect on my life," or "This works for me," you're in denial. It's not that you can't turn over a new leaf – you're so resistant right now that you just won't.

You're playing it safe. Be honest with yourself – the life you're living right now is not truly the life that you want. The way things are functioning around you is not what you desire. Maybe you're afraid to try. Maybe you are afraid to fail. My friend, the only way you fail at something is to not try in the first place. Ever hear the saying, "You get an A for effort?" Stop settling for good enough and live the life you truly want to live.

Consider the possibility that the dysfunction in your life is wreaking havoc and affecting your focus, decision making, behavior, and overall well-being. At some point you need to do something about this. You are your responsibility. Things are going to shift and change for the better when you begin to change yourself, how you think, and what you do.

6 to 10: Stuck

If you answered "yes" to six to ten of these questions you're stuck. You actually spend time thinking about change, but you have not made up your mind to make the change. You're both willing and not willing at the same time, which creates conflicting feelings and causes confusion. Neither hot nor cold on the issue, you're standing dead center between the advantages and disadvantages of change: "I'd like to change, but I don't want to lose anything or anyone in the process"; "I know I should get it together, but I don't think I can commit"; "I want to, but I just haven't got around to it yet."

In considering the pros and cons you realize you're going to have to sacrifice, and it makes you uneasy. You're not trying to move in one direction or the other. I get it. You're attached to people, places, and things. You're not willing to give up any of it to do what needs to be done. You're not making the attempt because you're afraid of what you're going to have to give up in the process.

This mental state of mind you're in means there's no movement. You're going nowhere beneficial to your goals in life as long as you're standing still on the issue. Stop procrastinating. Do what you need to do now. You don't know if tomorrow is going to come; why put things off till then? Do you want things to continue not to get better? Do you? What do you want? Make a decision to move into action. You must make up your mind. Tell yourself you're no longer going to accept being stuck and wiggle your way out of indecisiveness. Get out of that ditch and do what needs to be done to give your "self" flexibility and freedom to move around.

My friend, it's hard to reach when you're stuck. When you're free, you have the ability to take action and promote change. I want you to remember four things:

1. You cannot take stuff with you when you're gone from this earth
2. You're your responsibility. People can't change you for you.
3. You have what it takes to get it done.
4. You are loved regardless of where you're at in life.

11 to 19: Busy

If you scored eleven to nineteen points, you're ready; however, you're busy. You're serious about turning over a new leaf and intend to do so. You are tired of things being the way they are. You actually want things to flow and function better in your life. You have wiggled your way out of the ditch and are committed to change. However, although you're ready and willing to take action and believe you have what it takes, you can't find enough time in the day to work on you – or you lack the know-how. No problem. This book will help you with that.

There are serious self - and time-management issues here. You can't seem to find the time for you with school, work, taking care of family, and socializing with friends as top priorities. Don't run yourself into the ground. Small changes have big results. Instead of going out with your friends, invite them over to help you get it together. Don't be embarrassed –- just make it fun for both you and them. You're going to have to find the time somewhere.

Say it out loud!

To have it, I must take the time for myself to do it.

20 to 28: Determined

Pat yourself on the back if you're in this number range. You're determined to do whatever it takes. You're fed up with the mess of your life as it is at the moment. You've reached your breaking point. You've said, "Enough is enough!" Not only are you committed to making a change, you're willing to turn over a new leaf. You're taking action now! You've realized you were only hurting yourself. The "good enough" attitude no longer cuts it. You are taking your life back! You and the way things function around you are your priorities. My friend, good for you! Keep working at it. Keep going! There's no turning back now.

Many people think it's too late to take their life back. They don't even try to! Not you, you're determined. Even if you don't know how to do something, you're willing to do your research and apply it. You don't care how much time it's going to take; you don't care what you're going to have to sacrifice. No, you know you'll have to lose to gain. You know what you want, and you're not willing to settle for anything less than that. You're giving old habits the cold shoulder. You're making change happen for you. I'm proud of you, my friend. Now, turn over a new leaf!

Note to the tester

The results do not matter. If you feel like you're ready, then you're ready. Now is your chance to fix the issues and spring into action. I've done some of the work for you; however, you'll have to implement the lessons and ideas of this book in your own life. Believe me when I tell you it's possible. My life was a "hot mess." I had to turn over leaf after leaf after leaf. I'm still turning over leaves. My friend, don't be surprised when you get it wrong more than a few times before you get it right. It's a part of the process. You're worth so much more than you know. Take the time and get it done. Commit to you. You have what it takes. You have the courage, you have the strength, you have the talent, and you're capable of achieving your goal(s). I don't care what "they" say, and you shouldn't either. That diagnosis is not an excuse to settle in life. I believe your better days are ahead. I'm speaking about good health. I am speaking about better finances. I am speaking about the life you desire and deserve.

Take Your Life Back

"You can't just hope for happy endings. You have to believe in them. Then do the work, take the risks."

~Nora Roberts

Write a Letter to Your Past

Dear Past,

Mon	**Tue**	**Wed**	**Thr**	**Fri**	**Sat**	**Sun**	Date: _____
○	○	○	○	○	○	○	

My goal(s):

My obstacle(s):

Plan to overcome obstacle(s):

Task to overcome each obstacle:

My hopes for the future:

Visualization (I see myself there already)

It looks like
_____

It feels like
_____

I see
_____

I hear
_____

Consistant with my dreams? **Yes/No**

Resources needed:

Skills I have that will help me accomplish my goal:

30 / 31 DAYS WITH SHAN

Positive affirmation:

My past failures resulted from
_____

Because
_____

Lesson learned
_____

Things to remember:

I will
_____

I will not
_____

I want
_____

I don't want
_____

I am
_____

I am not
_____

Because
_____

I will reward myself:

I _____ am commiting to myself this day of _____ year _____ to do the best I can possibly do while being the best I can possibly be in order to achieve my goal. I **WILL** reach my goal by _____, after which I will reward myself with the above for a job well done.

Signature_____ Witness_____

Results:

( ) Reward claimed   Date claimed

DAY 1
Humble Yourself

People often associate being humble with a person's confidence. I don't agree. You have a right to be confident in God-given talents and abilities. However, you should remain humble. In my opinion, knowing yourself is the best way to humble yourself. You have to know your own strengths, limits, and weaknesses. You have to know your importance in a matter – or lack thereof. You have to know when to bow down and when to stand up. You have to know when to stay and when to leave.

My friend, to humble yourself, you must surrender to what is now and prepare modestly for what will be. You accept what you cannot change in the moment. See things for what they are and not what they appear to be.

A humble person is not vain. They do not boast about fine cars, large houses, or fancy clothes. They understand material things are temporary things. They'd rather make an inward purchase of love – because it's lasting. They'd rather invest in others – and it's rewarding. Yes, a humble person is a person of service. They're willing to lay down their lives for the sake of others. They're givers of good gifts. Some aren't modest in appearance, but there's humility in their hearts. Some are modest in appearance, yet there's deception on their lips. Wisdom is justified of her children, my friends.

Humble people strive for no earthly thing for their own gain. If and when they strive, it's for the benefit of others. No. They're not without fault or sin, and they know this. They're not better or too good, and they accept this. My friend, I encourage you to humble yourself. Continue your fight with ego. Remain focused on what matters: Love. For love is your strength and your sword. With it, you can break chains and pierce through the heart of darkness.

No worries, my friend. Keep working on you. Keep doing what you're doing. It's hard to ignore the wind when it's slamming doors and breaking windows, but this too shall pass. Get ready, be ready, and stay ready. Your season's about to change. When it changes, make sure you prepare and work accordingly.

Embrace Humility

"Pride is concerned with who is right.
Humility is concerned with what is right."

~Ezra Taft Benson.

Embracing Humility

Fill in the blanks and then read the entire statement out loud.

I admit that I am not the best at _____ and that I'm limited in _____; However, it doesn't mean I have to abandon my dreams. I can continue to improve on _____ and learn how to _____ by _____, and I will ask _____ for help when help is needed and will respect, thank, recognize, and appreciate those who help me on my path to success. In the past I've judged others based on _____ because of _____, which caused them to _____ and me to _____ because _____. I will stop comparing myself to _____ and will no longer allow _____ to interfere with _____ and will do my best to _____. Instead of judging them, I will separate my opinions from my fears to judge myself and think of ways I can improve instead of ways I think others should act. I cannot control other people's _____, but I can control my own _____. I am grateful for _____ and that _____ because _____. I am not afraid to _____ and understand that I will make mistakes because

I am not perfect, although I strive for perfection. I will admit my mistakes rather than trying to cover them up, regardless of my emotional state. I will sustain a healthy self-esteem and will be proud of my accomplishments, but I will not brag to bring attention to myself or my achievements. I will be considerate and mindful of others and will not talk down to or disrupt anyone. I will respect everyone's opinions, goals, and dreams — even if they are not consistent with my own. I'm fully aware that I don't know_____as much as I think I do and that others may know just as much if not more. For this reason, I will do my best to remain teachable and amazed by even the smallest of things. When I feel the need to be first, I will deliberately go last. I will give compliments just because, listen more than I talk, and will apologize as needed. I will practice _____and will be_____with myself because _____.

Add Your Own:

_____
_____
_____
_____

Mon	**Tue**	**Wed**	**Thr**	**Fri**	**Sat**	**Sun**	Date: _____
○	○	○	○	○	○	○	

My goal(s):

My obstacle(s):

Plan to overcome obstacle(s):

Task to overcome each obstacle:

My hopes for the future:

Visualization (I see myself there already)

It looks like
_____
It feels like
_____
I see
_____
I hear
_____

Consistant with my dreams? **Yes/No**

Resources needed:

Skills I have that will help me accomplish my goal:

Positive affirmation:

My past failures resulted from
_____

Because
_____

Lesson learned
_____

Things to remember:

I will
_____

I will not
_____

I want
_____

I don't want
_____

I am
_____

I am not
_____

Because
_____

I will reward myself:

I _____ am commiting to myself this day of _____ year _____ to do the best I can possibly do while being the best I can possibly be in order to achieve my goal. I **WILL** reach my goal by _____, after which I will reward myself with the above for a job well done.

Signature_____ Witness_____

Results:

( ) Reward claimed   Date claimed

DAY 2
Break the Habit

You can't keep doing what you're doing. You have to break the habit. Break it like a piggy bank. Get something out of it you can use to get what you want. Take the time to think about it, my love. Think about what it is you really want. Then think about what it's going to take for you to get it. It's going to cost you something – time, energy, friends, money, comfort. Believe me when I tell you it's not going to come free, and it won't be easy.

You're going to have to work to earn this. You're going to have to be open and honest with yourself and others. At times, you may feel like you've lost your mind. No, you're not crazy, my love. You're determined to do better. There's going to be times when you just want to throw in the towel. Times when you want to give up. Times when you feel like you're not equipped. Times when you feel like you're not enough. Times when you feel like you're chicken – running around with your head cut off. Don't let this stop you, my love.

Your determination will get you there. Keep looking towards your future. If you can see it, you can be it. Things aren't always going to make sense. Take time to figure it out. This is when you'll begin to understand. You need to get motivated. You need to get excited about your future. Make strides my love. Make strides towards your success. Let your light SHINE...and burst through this darkness.

I know, it can be hard to break the habit. I have a few I'm smashing myself. Nonetheless my friend, it can be broken. Addictions do not last unless you want them to. You're not defeated until you give up. Running away doesn't mean you'll get away. Stand there and face it, my love. Face you.

You're the only one standing in your way. Don't buckle under pressure; build up. Build up...and then explode in success. You may have to be alone for a spell. You may have to get away from distraction in order to become the attraction. Do you understand?

Do what it takes to get to where you want to be in life. You already have what it takes. "Sweep around your own front door." Stop judging what they do...and start focusing on what you're doing. Be humble. Be forgiving.

My friend, it happened, but you're still breathing. There's still life in your body. You still have time to change. You still have time to take your life back. When you break this bad habit, throw those pieces of bitterness away. They won't do you any good.

There's no use going back to where you've already come from. That house is infested. My love, break the habit. Get something out of it you can use. Pack up your belongings and then move on from it.

Move in Action to Your Destiny

Note to Self:

"Feeling sorry for yourself, and your present condition, is not only a waste of energy but the worst habit you could possibly have."

~Dale Carnegie

Breaking Bad Habits

Identify negative habits to promote positive change.

I have a habit of
___

Positive   Good   Bad   Crippling   Damaging   Hindering   Negative   Other
   ○   ○   ○   ○   ○   ○   ○   _____

Conscious Habit   Not Conscious   Productive   Unproductive
      ○   ○   ○   ○

Physical   Mental   Emotional   Social   Occupational   Sexual   Other
   ○   ○   ○   ○   ○   ○   _____

What feeling(s) is/are associated with the behavior?
___

What are the triggers for this habit?
___

Is maintaining this habit allowing you to cope with or avoid something unpleasant? **Yes/No**

What is the origin of the behavior?
___

What do you get from this habit?
___

Is it affecting your health and well-being? **Yes/No**

Physical   Mental   Emotional   Social   Occupational   Other
   ○   ○   ○   ○   ○   ○   _____

Positive substitute for the bad behavior
___

Accountability partner for this habit

Name_____ Phone_____

Breaking Bad Habits

Identify negative habits to promote positive change.

I have a habit of

Positive   Good   Bad   Crippling   Damaging   Hindering   Negative   Other
  ○   ○   ○   ○   ○   ○   ○   _____

Conscious Habit   Not Conscious   Productive   Unproductive
     ○   ○   ○   ○

Physical   Mental   Emotional   Social   Occupational   Sexual   Other
   ○   ○   ○   ○   ○   ○   _____

What feeling(s) is/are associated with the behavior?

_____

What are the triggers for this habit?

_____

Is maintaining this habit allowing you to cope with or avoid something unpleasant? **Yes/No**

What is the origin of the behavior?

_____

What do you get from this habit?

_____

Is it affecting your health and well-being? **Yes/No**

Physical   Mental   Emotional   Social   Occupational   Other
   ○   ○   ○   ○   ○   ○   _____

Positive substitute for the bad behavior

_____

Accountability partner for this habit

Name_____Phone_____

Turning over a new leaf / 45

| **Mon** | **Tue** | **Wed** | **Thr** | **Fri** | **Sat** | **Sun** | Date: _____ |
| O | O | O | O | O | O | O | |

My goal(s):

My obstacle(s):

Plan to overcome obstacle(s):

Task to overcome each obstacle:

My hopes for the future:

Visualization (I see myself there already)

It looks like
_____

It feels like
_____

I see
_____

I hear
_____

Consistant with my dreams? **Yes/No**

Resources needed:

Skills I have that will help me accomplish my goal:

Positive affirmation:

My past failures resulted from _____

Because _____

Lesson learned _____

Things to remember:

I will _____

I will not _____

I want _____

I don't want _____

I am _____

I am not _____

Because _____

I will reward myself: _____

I _____ am commiting to myself this day of _____ year _____ to do the best I can possibly do while being the best I can possibly be in order to achieve my goal. I **WILL** reach my goal by _____, after which I will reward myself with the above for a job well done.

Signature_____ Witness_____

Results:

( ) Reward claimed   Date claimed

DAY 3
Don't Fight the End

Whether it's the ending of a good movie, relationship, or a good song...I hate when it's over. I want to stay in the moment. I want to keep enjoying things the way they are... even when they're not enjoyable. Wait! What? Yes, I like torturing myself...not! Let's do it together. Let's let the end be the end and embrace new beginnings.

How long are you seriously going to let people continue to insult your intelligence? How long are you going to continue to let them use you when you don't want to be used? How long are you going to continue to allow them to treat you as if you're nobody? As if you're beneath them? You don't have that many cheeks to turn. While you're turning cheeks, they're turning their nose up at you. They don't think you're good enough for them. Truth be told, my love, they're not good enough for you. Don't ever forget that!

You are treasure to be found. Blessed is the one who finds you. Blessed is the one who knows how to handle you. Blessed is the one who knows how to treat and take care of you. You'll make them rich! My love, know your worth. You're worth more than what they're making you think you're worth. You're not pyrite. You're gold. You're not glass in the sand. You're a diamond.

You cannot control the end. Just let it happen. It's a sign of new beginnings. Don't let this get you down. Take care of you. Eat and be merry. It's really not that serious. You'll laugh about it later. Learn from this. Don't fall for it again. Looks can be deceiving. Don't focus on what's on the outside. Shit can come wrapped in a nice package. Nonetheless, it is... what it is...-and it stinks.

Take your time. Get more information. There's no rush. Man's time is illusion, God's Time is reality. Follow your first mind. If you think someone has ulterior motives, go with that.

You have a natural GPS built inside of you called spirit. Follow directions, and you'll arrive where you need to be when you need to be – on time. Don't go against the flow. Surrender. Let go. Stop wasting time. The credits are already rolling...

Let this End to Begin

"When I let go of what I am, I become what I might be. When I let go of what I have, I receive what I need."

~Lao Tzu

Are you fighting the end?
Take the test below to see if you're ready to move on.

1. Do you fantasize about the past in regards to the person, place, situation, circumstance, or thing?
   Yes ( )   No ( )   Sometimes ( )

2. Are you doing things differently than what you've done in the past to impress the person, place, situation, circumstance, or thing?
   Yes ( )   No ( )   Sometimes ( )

3. Do you think of the person, place, situation, circumstance, or thing even when you don't want to?
   Yes ( )   No ( )   Sometimes ( )

4. Are you ready to move on regardless of how it affects the person, place, situation, circumstance, or thing?
   Yes ( )   No ( )   Sometimes ( )

5. Are you ready to make a change even if it may temporarily cause conflict?
   Yes ( )   No ( )   Sometimes ( )

6. Are you ready to block out anyone that does not respect or support your efforts?
   Yes ( )   No ( )   Sometimes ( )

7. Are you tired of being unhappy in life?
   Yes ( )   No ( )   Sometimes ( )

8. Do thoughts of this person, place, situation, circumstance, or thing comfort you when you're feeling down?
   Yes ( )   No ( )   Sometimes ( )

9. Do you wonder about what could have been or one day may be between you and the subject?
    Yes ( )   No ( )   Sometimes ( )

10. Do you blame for the way things turned out?
    Yes ( )   No ( )   Sometimes ( )

11. Do thoughts of this person, place, situation, circumstance, or thing trigger an emotional reaction?
    Yes ( )   No ( )   Sometimes ( )

12. Do you seek approval from the subject?
    Yes ( )   No ( )   Sometimes ( )

13. Do you wish you could get revenge or find ways to make the subject regret whatever happened?
    Yes ( )   No ( )   Sometimes ( )

14. Do you find ways to bring your subject up in conversations?
    Yes ( )   No ( )   Sometimes ( )

15. Do you feel the need to contact, visit, or connect with the subject and often do so even when you try not to?
    Yes ( )   No ( )   Sometimes ( )

Calculate your score

How many "yes" answers do you have? _____

0 to 4: You have moved on!
5 to 10: You're ready, but something's holding you back.
10 to 15: You're fighting the end.

Mon	Tue	Wed	Thr	Fri	Sat	Sun	Date: _____
○	○	○	○	○	○	○	

My goal(s):

My obstacle(s):

Plan to overcome obstacle(s):

Task to overcome each obstacle:

My hopes for the future:

Visualization (I see myself there already)

It looks like
_____

It feels like
_____

I see
_____

I hear
_____

Consistant with my dreams? **Yes/No**

Resources needed:

Skills I have that will help me accomplish my goal:

Positive affirmation:

My past failures resulted from
_____

Because
_____

Lesson learned
_____

Things to remember:

I will
_____

I will not
_____

I want
_____

I don't want
_____

I am
_____

I am not
_____

Because
_____

I will reward myself:

I _____ am commiting to myself this day of _____ year _____ to do the best I can possibly do while being the best I can possibly be in order to achieve my goal. I **WILL** reach my goal by _____, after which I will reward myself with the above for a job well done.

Signature_____ Witness_____

Results:

( ) Reward claimed   Date claimed

DAY 4
Learn When to Stop

Sometimes a cautious halt is wise. Sometimes STOP is required. You might crash if you keep on going. This is one of those times. Not all roads have stop signs on them; however, this particular road does. Stop and make a turn to the right. There's a dead end the direction you're going. Make the turn. You don't want to miss out on your blessing because you're going the wrong way. You don't want to miss out on that "good" man or woman...chasing behind that "bad" man... or woman. You don't want to neglect good friends...while traveling to pick up fake friends.

Make the turn. Make sure you don't miss anything you're supposed to see. I know, it's easy to start, but it's hard to finish. It makes you feel like you're giving up on something or someone. My friend, don't worry about their feelings in this matter. They didn't think about your feelings when they treated you that way. They didn't think about your feelings when they saw you walking and kept going. They didn't even bother to wave. This way, they can claim they didn't see you. They will never see you, my love. They see what they want to see. They see only what they want to take from you. This is a part of the problem. It should be a give-and-take relationship. Not a take-take-take.

Have that conversation you've been putting off. You'll be glad you did. I know it's annoying. You just want to get to a place filled with love, to find peace and rest. You just want a place to call home. My love, you'll get there sooner than expected once you start going in the right direction. Don't freak out. Stay calm. Pay attention. Breathe!

You should always be prepared for delay and distraction. Little dove, this is distraction not delay. You're just on the wrong road. No matter how you approach this STOP sign, just make sure you make the stop.

Follow your heart home. You already know how to get there. You're just being stubborn. You're playing a game that's already lost. Deep down, you know this.

Lately, you've been getting overwhelmed by all the construction around you. Some people can't avoid it. Some people have no choice but to be delayed by drama. My friend, you're lucky. You can get around it. Stop and make the turn.

The road you're supposed to be on is already finished. It's already done. It's beautiful: filled with irresistible, eye-catching things. They're not already claimed. You can park the car, go get it, and say, "This is mine," and it will be yours. That's how easy it's going to be once you turn right.

Don't pass by your opportunity to change direction, my love. Don't keep allowing yourself to be distracted by drama and temptation. Make the turn.

Go Get the Life You Want

Note to Self:

"You gain strength, courage, and confidence by every experience in which you really stop to look fear in the face. You must do the thing you think you cannot do."

~Eleanor Roosevelt

Turning over a new leaf / 59

35 Stop Signs

Drop a small object on this page with your eyes closed. The number(s) the object covers is/are the thing(s) you should stop doing. Use the next page to find out what the numbers on each stop sign represent.

Find the number(s) your object landed on and read what you're being encouraged to stop doing.

1. Running away
2. Lying to self
3. Obsessing
4. Negativity
5. Distraction
6. Selfishness
7. Overthinking
8. Hoarding
9. Denial
10. Criticizing
11. Comparing
12. Procrastining
13. Complaining
14. Being afraid
15. Trying to be perfect
16. Neglecting self
17. Jealousy
18. Wasting time
19. Living in the past
20. Being controlling
21. Feeling sorry for self
22. Trying to fix it
23. Unhealthy habits
24. Wasting money
25. Settling
26. Repeating the cycle
27. Listening to "them"
28. Hanging with "them"
29. Expecting people to
30. Being unforgiving
31. Worrying
32. Blaming
33. Harming
34. Being ungrateful
35. Letting "them" treat you that way

Mon	**Tue**	**Wed**	**Thr**	**Fri**	**Sat**	**Sun**	Date: _____
○	○	○	○	○	○	○	

My goal(s):

My obstacle(s):

Plan to overcome obstacle(s):

Task to overcome each obstacle:

My hopes for the future:

Visualization (I see myself there already)

It looks like
_____

It feels like
_____

I see
_____

I hear
_____

Consistant with my dreams? **Yes/No**

Resources needed:

Skills I have that will help me accomplish my goal:

Positive affirmation:

My past failures resulted from
_____

Because
_____

Lesson learned
_____

Things to remember:

I will
_____

I will not
_____

I want
_____

I don't want
_____

I am
_____

I am not
_____

Because
_____

I will reward myself:

I _____ am commiting to myself this day of _____ year _____ to do the best I can possibly do while being the best I can possibly be in order to achieve my goal. I **WILL** reach my goal by _____, after which I will reward myself with the above for a job well done.

Signature_____ Witness_____

Results:

( ) Reward claimed   Date claimed

DAY 5
Can't Change Them

It won't work. People only change when they want to change. People only change when they think they're ready to change. It doesn't matter what you know about them. What you see in them won't matter until they see for themselves. They will not make any commitment to be different than who they are right now – until they begin to see themselves differently. You can express your opinion as long as you know it's your opinion. Otherwise, keep it to yourself.

Your view will always come second to their view. They can't see what you see. They're blinded by the issues of bad circumstance. What can you do? My friend, you can lead by example. You can make life look so good...that others beg you for a piece of what you have. You won't have to go find them. They'll seek you out.

Stop trying to change people. You were not put on this earth to judge...I don't care who you think you are. You're here to love. Therefore, love is your duty to this person. Love them unconditionally. This doesn't mean let them treat you any kind of way. Don't do that. You can love from a distance.

I don't know why and how you expect these people to love you when they don't even know how to love themselves (yet). Don't get down on their level. Don't dive in the mud to play dirty. My friend, you have been cleansed already. You don't have anything to prove. Let time do your telling. Don't say a word; know the word. Remember what was promised to you, little dove. Start walking according to this promise, knowing it's already been done.

Accept what you need to accept from this situation and move on. Stop wasting your time. Don't let distraction build a wall between you and your destiny. Start taking care of you.

You give your all...and you lose it all... Why? My friend, it only appears that you've lost. Losing at times is required for winning. Sometimes you have to lose to gain. Take this time to learn how to balance on the beam of life. Don't get too comfortable where you are. When thoughts of the past come rushing in like a flood, remember, you have a Lifesaver.

Change You in Relation to Them

"If you don't like something, change it. If you can't change it, change your attitude."

~Maya Angelou

Finding the Solution

Use this exercise to help promote change in others. Think of a person you'd like to promote a behavioral change in and answer the following questions.

Is the person open to suggestions? **Yes/No**

If no, they don't take well to others "telling" them what to do. Don't waste your time. Find creative ways to promote change.

Does the person make negative fixed statements about self? **Yes/No**
If yes, he/she may not think it's possible to change. However, all is not lost. They want to change but haven't figured out how to change. You may be able to help them.

What is the exact behavior you want to change?
___
___
___

How do you want it to change?
___
___
___
___

Are you willing to accept this person if the behavior doesn't change? **Yes/No**

Research the behavior. Why do they do it?
___
___
___
___
___
___
___

What positive feedback are you going to give this person?
_____
_____

How can you limit or prevent the behavior?
_____
_____

Inform the person the behavior bothers you. Be calm and substitute "You're the one that" statements with "I feel like" statements.

Practice:

When you _____
I feel like_____, and that _____me.
For example, when _____. Next time _____,
could you please _____.

What was the person's response?
_____
_____

Did you make your feelings about the behavior clear? **Yes/No**
If yes, How?
_____
_____

What information did you give the person about the behavior that will encourage them to change it?
_____
_____

How will you reward the person for good behavior?
_____
_____
_____
_____

Mon   Tue   Wed   Thr   Fri   Sat   Sun   Date: _____
 ○   ○   ○   ○   ○   ○   ○

My goal(s):

My obstacle(s):

Plan to overcome obstacle(s):

Task to overcome each obstacle:

My hopes for the future:

Visualization (I see myself there already)

It looks like
_____
It feels like
_____
I see
_____
I hear
_____
Consistant with my dreams? **Yes/No**

Resources needed:

Skills I have that will help me accomplish my goal:

Positive affirmation:

My past failures resulted from
_____

Because
_____

Lesson learned
_____

Things to remember:

I will
_____

I will not
_____

I want
_____

I don't want
_____

I am
_____

I am not
_____

Because
_____

I will reward myself:

I _____ am commiting to myself this day of _____ year _____ to do the best I can possibly do while being the best I can possibly be in order to achieve my goal. I **WILL** reach my goal by _____, after which I will reward myself with the above for a job well done.

Signature_____ Witness_____

Results:

( ) Reward claimed   Date claimed

DAY 6
Don't Feel Bad

You can't help anyone until you help yourself. To do this, it's often required that you get to yourself. You have work to do. You've rested long enough. Don't let people make you feel bad for taking care of you.

You have a good heart. You're always there for others. People use you as a crutch to lean on. My friend, most of the people you're allowing to lean on you are going to drop you like a bad habit once they heal. Take care of you first. You've spent your entire life giving and not receiving. You'd give your last dime, the last crumb you were about to lick off the floor underneath the table. No worries. The Great Spirit has your back.

Man cannot give you anything of true value. Even that which he gives, he'll one day take back. Strive to obtain gifts from God. They're lasting. The person you're worried about right now has someone else standing in their corner. It's just you and the Great Spirit. Guess what. At the end of the day, when it's all said and done, that's all you're ever going to need.

Stay committed to your goals. Don't get distracted by the nonsense. Have good sense. Don't let the waves of others drift you from your Goal. Most people don't achieve because they don't sacrifice. Dreaming is one thing, but my friend, you must wake up from that dream to make it a reality. You must sacrifice good sleep to go work on your life.

Continue to have positive outlook. Continue to be self-disciplined. Don't concern yourself with issues that don't belong to you. It's not your responsibility. You are responsible for you. You're responsible for your purpose. You're responsible for your assignment. It's your responsibility to become. People are waiting on you to get there. They can't move until you arrive. Do you understand?

You can't stay standing there. You're going to have to leave some people behind. This is okay. It's for now - not forever. Your life needs to improve. You can't wait for them. You just may have to step on a few toes to get to where you need to be. Say excuse me and keep it stepping.

My love, I know you're facing difficult decisions today. Don't back down. Stand your ground for achievement. Do what you have to do to get there. No, don't feel bad about it. People are waiting on you to arrive. Arrive on time, little dove. Arrive!

Take Care of Yourself

Note to Self:

"Remember, if you ever need a helping hand, it's at the end of your arm, as you get older, remember you have another hand: The first is to help yourself, the second is to help others."

~Audrey Hepburn

Helping Yourself First

Fill in the blanks and share with your accountability partner.

I feel negative about_____ because_____.
I feel positive about _____ because_____.
I'm grateful for_____ because_____.
I'm proud of myself for_____
because_____.

What things brought you pleasure today?
_____
_____
_____
_____
_____

What activities made you feel content?
_____
_____
_____
_____

Close your eyes. Think about the things that made you happy or content and then fill in the blanks below.

I sense _____
I feel _____
I see _____
I hear_____
I smell _____
I taste _____

What do the things that make you happy and the things that make you content have in common?
_____

In what location were you the happiest?
_____

When do you feel like you're doing and being your best?
_____

How many hours of sleep do you normally get? _____

Exercise is an important part of taking care of yourself. What's your workout plan?

_____
_____
_____
_____
_____

How much water do you drink a day? _____

What's your nutrition plan? You should eat at least three meals a day with healthy snacks in between.

_____
_____
_____
_____
_____

Keep track of your spending. What's your budget plan?

_____
_____
_____
_____
_____

Mon Tue Wed Thr Fri Sat Sun   Date: _____
 ○   ○   ○   ○   ○   ○   ○

My goal(s):

My obstacle(s):

Plan to overcome obstacle(s):

Task to overcome each obstacle:

My hopes for the future:

Visualization (I see myself there already)

It looks like
_____
It feels like
_____
I see
_____
I hear
_____
Consistant with my dreams? **Yes/No**

Resources needed:

Skills I have that will help me accomplish my goal:

Positive affirmation:

My past failures resulted from
_____

Because
_____

Lesson learned
_____

Things to remember:

I will
_____

I will not
_____

I want
_____

I don't want
_____

I am
_____

I am not
_____

Because
_____

I will reward myself:

I _____ am commiting to myself this day of _____ year _____ to do the best I can possibly do while being the best I can possibly be in order to achieve my goal. I **WILL** reach my goal by _____, after which I will reward myself with the above for a job well done.

Signature_____ Witness_____

Results:

( ) Reward claimed   Date claimed

DAY 7
You Owe Yourself

Too many people go through life mad at the world. Too many people blame everyone but themselves, thinking somebody owes them something. No, they don't owe you nothing. You owe yourself everything. You're your responsibility. There's no need to be angry and upset. Eat that chip off of your shoulder. Use this to get you there. You're not hurting them. They're sleeping good at night.

You're hurting you. Nothing happens to you without reason. You may not have had a perfect childhood. The people raising you may not have done a good job. Maybe you've been laid off from work. Use this to get you there. Learn from those bad parents how to be a good parent. See this layoff as opportunity for promotion – apply for a better job.

Don't settle. You're worth so much more than you're giving yourself. Stop making up excuses to be bitter. Stop making excuses. Take the knife out of that wound. Allow yourself to heal from this. Forgive. Not for them. Do it for you!

My friend, you can't keep this. Let it go! Don't think this is all life has to offer you. No, my love, there's balance and order.

If your start was ugly, it's because you're destined to have a beautiful finish. You're not being cheated. You're being setup for your good. The Great Spirit is trying to help you get to where you're supposed to be. You're not supposed to be in a negative space. Why are you still there? Why are you still standing in the same place? MOVE...from this.

Yes, you were wronged, you were betrayed, and you feel pain, but if you take the knife out, you can heal from this. If you start making steps towards the life you want...you'll have a new beginning. It takes one step forward to begin again, my friend. You can start now. Start by saying, _____, I forgive you. You don't have to tell them. Tell you. Just make sure you forgive yourself.

Do whatever you can to get over this, my love, and move forward. Beautiful things are waiting for you in the distance. You just have to get to them.

You're Deserving and Worth It

"You may have had unfair things happen, but know that the depth of your pain is an indication of the height of your future."

~Joel Osteen

Write a Letter to Yourself

Dear Past,

Mon	Tue	Wed	Thr	Fri	Sat	Sun	Date: _____
○	○	○	○	○	○	○	

My goal(s):

My obstacle(s):

Plan to overcome obstacle(s):

Task to overcome each obstacle:

My hopes for the future:

Visualization (I see myself there already)

It looks like

It feels like

I see

I hear

Consistant with my dreams? **Yes/No**

Resources needed:

Skills I have that will help me accomplish my goal:

Positive affirmation:

My past failures resulted from

_____

Because

_____

Lesson learned

_____

Things to remember:

I will

_____

I will not

_____

I want

_____

I don't want

_____

I am

_____

I am not

_____

Because

_____

I will reward myself:

I _____ am commiting to myself this day of _____ year _____ to do the best I can possibly do while being the best I can possibly be in order to achieve my goal. I **WILL** reach my goal by _____, after which I will reward myself with the above for a job well done.

Signature_____ Witness_____

Results:

( ) Reward claimed   Date claimed

DAY 8
Don't Need Them To

My friend, you don't need them to do what you're supposed to be doing. You don't need them to agree. You don't need them to like it. You don't need them to like you. You just need them to hear it. You just need them to see it. Don't do it for them. Do it for you. Don't give to expect. You'll only set yourself up to be disappointed. When you give, give from the heart.

Two things will be most beneficial at this time: giving and forgiving. Now, when I say giving, in your case, I'm talking about giving to you. Yes, my love, you deserve some of that too. You deserve some of that love. You deserve some of that attention. Most importantly...You Deserve. It's time for you to shift gears a bit. You can't depend on them. You can't rely on them. And you definitely shouldn't expect them to.

Nothing new under the sun, my love. There's been no change. You haven't made progress. Why? Because you're expecting others to do for you...what you should be doing for yourself. No one is going to take care of you better than you. You know when you're hurt. Others only know after the fact.

After you've shown signs. After you tell them. Or they just assume. You know right away!

My friend, you're hurting. You're hurting yourself. Stop it! Just stop! "But Shan, I wasn't raised by my mother. My father was never there. They beat me. He cheated on me. They took this, and they done that." I hear you.

I know what It feels like to want to be wanted. To fit in somewhere. To call a place home. To be loved, accepted, and allowed to be me. I know what it feels like to be misunderstood. I know what it feels like to be mistreated. I know what it feels like to live in a cage. I lived there for years...until I realized the door was open.

My friend, the door to that cage is open. You can fly out anytime you get ready. You don't have to wait on someone to take you out...just to put you back in. You don't need them to do for you what you can do for yourself.

Fly away from this, my love. Go get the life you want. There's a reason...I promise you there is a reason these things have happened. It's going to be for your good. It's going to work out in your favor – if you let it.

Free Yourself

"Emancipate yourselves from mental slavery.
None but ourselves can free our minds."

~Bob Marley

Fly out of the Cage

The door to the cage has been left open. Use the next page to free yourself.

1 Pay attention to your thoughts	**2** Challenge your thinking	**3** Become aware	**Love** Practice selflessness
4 Confront your ego	**5** Express yourself	**6** Focus on the now	**7** Learn from living
8 Practice gratitude	**9** Stop expecting others to	**10** Explore your boundaries	**11** Break the habit
12 Remove the blocks or make them useful	**13** Relinquish control	**14** Don't attach to material things	**15** Don't worry about what "they" think
16 Dispose of the toxic relationship	**17** Purge the unnecessary	**Hope** Be positive	**18** Forgive
19 Process your grief	**20** Don't stop trying	**Fly** Make the effort	**Freedom**

| **Mon** | **Tue** | **Wed** | **Thr** | **Fri** | **Sat** | **Sun** | Date: _____ |
| ○ | ○ | ○ | ○ | ○ | ○ | ○ | |

My goal(s):

My obstacle(s):

Plan to overcome obstacle(s):

Task to overcome each obstacle:

My hopes for the future:

Visualization (I see myself there already)

It looks like
_____

It feels like
_____

I see
_____

I hear
_____

Consistant with my dreams? **Yes/No**

Resources needed:

Skills I have that will help me accomplish my goal:

Positive affirmation:

My past failures resulted from
_____

Because
_____

Lesson learned
_____

Things to remember:

I will
_____

I will not
_____

I want
_____

I don't want
_____

I am
_____

I am not
_____

Because
_____

I will reward myself:

I _____ am commiting to myself this day of _____ year _____ to do the best I can possibly do while being the best I can possibly be in order to achieve my goal. I **WILL** reach my goal by _____, after which I will reward myself with the above for a job well done.

Signature_____ Witness_____

Results:

( ) Reward claimed   Date claimed

DAY 9
Because You Can

Just because you can, it doesn't mean you should. We have to do better. There's good and bad inside each of us. One says, "I will treat others the way I would like to be treated. I will care for those who cannot care for themselves. I will love in spite of." The other says, "You gotta be out your mind... Curse them out!!! You better get them before they get you. You gone sit there and take that?" One wants to bend. The other wants to break. My friend, don't let your emotions make this decision for you.

It's easy to bend something back in place; it's hard to put something back together once it's broken. When something breaks, a bond is severed. Something shared to make a whole ceases to exist. Only a mess remains. You have a choice. I encourage you to choose good. I encourage you to smile and greet your neighbors well. I encourage you to not criticize or complain. I encourage you to be patient with one another. We're all on a journey.

You don't have to step on someone to get to where you're going. If it's destined...you'll get there regardless. You don't have to flip that person off. You don't have to roll your eyes and smack your lips. You don't have to take advantage of others. You don't have to be mean and nasty...just to be mean and nasty. It's not doing the world any good.

The world is a beautiful place filled with ugly people. It's not supposed to be this way. No, my friends, take advantage of opportunity...not each other. How can something so beautiful be so ugly?

My friend, once you break trust, you can pick up all the pieces...but you won't be able to bond like before. Don't do it. Behind every great person are other smart, talented, and intelligent people. Be that great person. Do good. Be good. Choose good.

Don't Exploit Weakness

Note to Self:
___
___
___
___
___
___
___

"Our prime purpose in this life is to help others. And if you can't help them, at least don't hurt them."

~Bob Marley

Are You "Using" Others?

Take the test below to see if you're taking advantage.

1. Do you only reach out to others when you're in need of something?
   Yes ( )   No ( )   Sometimes ( )

2. Do you tell secrets that others have entrusted to you without their permission?
   Yes ( )   No ( )   Sometimes ( )

3. Do you often exclude from social events those you've asked to do more than a few favors?
   Yes ( )   No ( )   Sometimes ( )

4. Do you often neglect to return favors as promised?
   Yes ( )   No ( )   Sometimes ( )

5. Are you genuinely NOT appreciative when someone helps you out?
   Yes ( )   No ( )   Sometimes ( )

6. Do you manipulate others with tactics to guilt trip them into doing things they don't want to do?
   Yes ( )   No ( )   Sometimes ( )

7. Do you always try to boss others around and tell them what to do, particularly for your benefit?
   Yes ( )   No ( )   Sometimes ( )

8. Has anyone ever accused you of using them?
   Yes ( )   No ( )   Sometimes ( )

9. Do you go out your way to make others feel uncomfortable?
   Yes ( )   No ( )   Sometimes ( )

10. Do you make people afraid to say no?
    Yes ( )   No ( )   Sometimes ( )

11. Are you only nice when it's convenient?
    Yes ( )   No ( )   Sometimes ( )

12. Do you focus on your needs and wants and not the needs and wants of others?
    Yes ( )   No ( )   Sometimes ( )

13. Do you rope others back in when they seem to get away from you?
    Yes ( )   No ( )   Sometimes ( )

14. Do you ever lie to get your way?
    Yes ( )   No ( )   Sometimes ( )

15. Are you a jealous person?
    Yes ( )   No ( )   Sometimes ( )

16. Do you often feel superior, entitled, or that others are beneath you?
    Yes ( )   No ( )   Sometimes ( )

Calculate your score

How many "yes" answers do you have? _____

0 to 1: You're not purposely taking advantage of others.
1 to 5: Sometimes you take advantage of others.
5 to 10: You often take advantage of others for your benefit.
10 to 16: You always take advantage of others and don't care.

Mon	**Tue**	**Wed**	**Thr**	**Fri**	**Sat**	**Sun**	Date: _____
○	○	○	○	○	○	○	

My goal(s):

My obstacle(s):

Plan to overcome obstacle(s):

Task to overcome each obstacle:

My hopes for the future:

Visualization (I see myself there already)

It looks like
_____
It feels like
_____
I see
_____
I hear
_____

Consistant with my dreams? **Yes/No**

Resources needed:

Skills I have that will help me accomplish my goal:

Positive affirmation: _____

My past failures resulted from
_____

Because
_____

Lesson learned
_____

Things to remember:

I will
_____

I will not
_____

I want
_____

I don't want
_____

I am
_____

I am not
_____

Because
_____

I will reward myself:

I _____ am commiting to myself this day of _____ year _____ to do the best I can possibly do while being the best I can possibly be in order to achieve my goal. I **WILL** reach my goal by _____, after which I will reward myself with the above for a job well done.

Signature_____ Witness_____

Results:

( ) Reward claimed   Date claimed

DAY 10
Don't Cross Wires

Someone's paying close attention to every move you make. This isn't necessarily a bad thing. It means they're learning something from you. What you choose to teach is up to you. You can teach them how to walk with their heads held high, or you can teach them to fear a fly on the wall.

Don't let the actions of others get to you. As long as you continue to make the right moves, in the end, you'll be okay. You've already won the game. Don't let people take you out of it! Don't let them take you out of you! This doesn't mean you have to keep silent about it. No, speak up! Some people just don't know. It's up to you to tell them. Don't put this off till next time. Do it now. It's up to you to teach them the right way. Show them by example.

Think about what you can learn from them, because they are defiantly learning something from you. You can learn something for sure – even if it's what not to do. I know it may be uncomfortable for you, my love, but being uncomfortable is sometimes necessary for healing and growth.

Relationships can be annoying, yet they're still important. There's always going to be challenge when you're dealing with more than one ego. You have a hard time just dealing with yours. Be open, my love. Don't write them off just yet. When you need them most, they'll be right by your side. I'm talking about those who are real, not that plastic stuff. Real friends are worth it. That's what you have, my love. You're not always going to agree. Be you…but let them be who they are.

Show them the way. You may have to help them out in this situation. Don't complain. Don't broadcast your sacrifice. They'll do more for you without even taking two seconds to think about it. Stop being selfish; invest in others. You'll get more than your "pennies" back down the line.

You may have been told, "Don't burn your bridges." I'm not going to tell you that. You're not even outside. I'm going to tell you not to cross your wires. Don't get caught up in a mess that could have been prevented in the first place. You can straighten this mess up right now. Clean it up! Stop fighting! Start communicating! Teach others how friends are supposed to interact.

My friend, take a moment to gather your thoughts. Think it through. Get advice – filter it, but get it. It'll help prepare you for this conversation. Just remember, my love, "Attitudes are contagious." If everyone's talking...it means nobody's listening.

Real Friends Are Worth It

Note to Self:

"Surround yourself with the dreamers and the doers, the believers and thinkers, but most of all, surround yourself with those who see greatness within you, even when you don't see it in yourself."

~Edmund Lee

Dealing with Conflict
Are you prepared to properly handle it?

What is your definition of conflict?
_____
_____
_____
_____

What is the dictionary's definition of conflict?
_____
_____
_____
_____
_____

How do you deal with conflict?
- a. I avoid it
- b. I accommodate it
- c. I compete
- d. I compromise
- e. I collaborate
- f. I cry

List 5 actions that could cause a conflict:
1. _____
2. _____
3. _____
4. _____
5. _____

List 5 reactions that intensify conflict:

1. _____
2. _____
3. _____
4. _____
5. _____

How do you plan to manage conflict in the future?

Mon	Tue	Wed	Thr	Fri	Sat	Sun	Date: _____
○	○	○	○	○	○	○	

My goal(s):

My obstacle(s):

Plan to overcome obstacle(s):

Task to overcome each obstacle:

My hopes for the future:

Visualization (I see myself there already)

It looks like
_____
It feels like
_____
I see
_____
I hear
_____
Consistant with my dreams? **Yes/No**

Resources needed:

Skills I have that will help me accomplish my goal:

Positive affirmation:

My past failures resulted from
_____

Because
_____

Lesson learned
_____

Things to remember:

I will
_____

I will not
_____

I want
_____

I don't want
_____

I am
_____

I am not
_____

Because
_____

I will reward myself:

I _____ am commiting to myself this day of _____ year _____ to do the best I can possibly do while being the best I can possibly be in order to achieve my goal. I **WILL** reach my goal by _____, after which I will reward myself with the above for a job well done.

Signature_____ Witness_____

Results:

( ) Reward claimed   Date claimed

DAY 11
Trash Is Treasure

Yes, their trash is your treasure. It's hard to let go of things you value. Others might encourage you to get rid of this and/or that, but as long as you've given that something or someone worth in your life, as long as you value a person, place, or thing, you'll do whatever you can to keep it and make sure it's safe. Why? Because he, she, or it is important to you.

What you value will have a place in your life regardless of what it looks like, regardless of what it feels like, regardless if it functions or not; regardless if it fits or not; regardless if it's being used or not. You love what you value, and when you love something or someone, you take further steps to protect it. Do you understand?

A person who doesn't value a person, place, and/or thing will simply leave the person, destroy the place, and trash the thing. Because, to them, he is not worth it. Because, to them, she is not worth it. Because, to them, it is not worth it!

You see, it's easy for some people to "just throw things away," things they consider not worth it. My friend, you're worth it! You have value! "They" just didn't know how to properly use you. "They" couldn't understand how to make you work for them.

My friend, this is not your fault. You have the looks, the strength, the personality, the right attitude, the talent, and the Resource. You have the heart to love them for who they are and the stomach to clean up their mess. No, it's not your fault; it's their "mistake."

They didn't see a masterpiece. They valued the frame and not the picture, so they threw you away like a piece of trash. My friend, good for you! Now you can be found by someone who's going to treat you right. Someone who's going to value you. Someone who's going to care for you. Someone who's going to protect you. Someone who's going to think you're worth it! No, someone who's going to know you are worth it!

You've heard it before, "One man's trash is another man's treasure." No, you're not garbage! You're not a waste of time! You're undiscovered treasure waiting to be found! My friend, you're going to make some lucky person rich one day. Instead of being perceived as small and inferior, – instead of being looked upon as damaged goods, – instead of being seen as something ordinary, – you're going to have extraordinary value. My friend, you're worth it! You are a masterpiece.

Don't settle for less than your worth. Where you are may be uncomfortable, with the stench of loneliness, the crowding of time, the waiting, and feelings of inadequacy, but don't lose hope. Be the best you can be – right where you are. Focus on you and not the things around you. Shine! Be confident! Be you! You are exactly what you've been looking for – love.

Don't Throw Away the Good Stuff

Note to Self:
_____
_____
_____
_____
_____
_____
_____
_____
_____
_____
_____
_____
_____
_____
_____

"The truth is, at any given moment, someone, somewhere, could be making a face about you,
but it's the reviews you give yourself that matter."

~Carrie Bradshaw

Building Self Worth

Fill in the blanks using only "Me," "Myself," and "I."

_____ am doing this because _____ need to understand the power of my attitude towards _____. How _____ perceive _____, how _____ talk about _____, and how _____ represent _____ eventually becomes my reality of self. _____ will not put _____ down. _____ will not belittle _____. _____ will not make fun of _____ to prevent others from doing so. _____ will be confident in _____ and my abilities to achieve. _____ am a valuable person. _____ am worthy. _____ am worth it! _____ value _____. _____ love _____ and am committed to being my own best friend. _____ will treat _____ with care. _____ will be tolerant with _____. _____ will be generous to _____. _____ will show _____ compassion and will not conform to the way _____ think others might perceive _____. _____ will not expect others to save _____ from _____ – because _____ know I'm the only one who can give _____ the boost _____ need to become _____. Therefore, _____ am ready and willing to face _____ and will not try to escape _____ through bad habits or addiction. _____ will listen to _____ and trust my gut feelings. _____ will accept _____ where _____ am for being who _____ am while striving to be the better _____. _____ will make decisions for _____. _____ will live, learn, and love for _____. _____ will not underestimate _____. _____ will tell _____ that _____ matter because _____ do. _____ will tell _____ that _____ am special because

____ am. ____ will tell _____ that ____ am lovable because ____ am. ____ will tell _____ that ____ am loved because ____ am. ____ will remain active in my life and take full responsibility for my actions. ____ will forgive _____ and will get through life's difficulties by not allowing _____ to fall apart. ____ will see all challenges as opportunity. ____ will express _____ and will not cower in a corner, because ____ am already victorious. ____ will make better life choices and financial decisions for _____. ____ will be happy, healthy and free to be ____. ____ will value _____ when no one else sees my value, because ____ am valuable.

How much are you worth to yourself? Why?

_____
_____
_____
_____
_____
_____

How much do you think you're worth to others? Why?

_____
_____
_____
_____
_____
_____

Mon	**Tue**	**Wed**	**Thr**	**Fri**	**Sat**	**Sun**	Date: _____
○	○	○	○	○	○	○	

My goal(s):

My obstacle(s):

Plan to overcome obstacle(s):

Task to overcome each obstacle:

My hopes for the future:

Visualization (I see myself there already)

It looks like
_____

It feels like
_____

I see
_____

I hear
_____

Consistant with my dreams? **Yes/No**

Resources needed:

Skills I have that will help me accomplish my goal:

Positive affirmation:

My past failures resulted from
_____

Because
_____

Lesson learned
_____

Things to remember:

I will
_____

I will not
_____

I want
_____

I don't want
_____

I am
_____

I am not
_____

Because
_____

I will reward myself:

I _____ am commiting to myself this day of _____ year _____ to do the best I can possibly do while being the best I can possibly be in order to achieve my goal. I **WILL** reach my goal by _____, after which I will reward myself with the above for a job well done.

Signature_____ Witness_____

Results:

( ) Reward claimed   Date claimed

DAY 12
This to Make That

Just because something looks broken doesn't mean it needs to be fixed. Those pieces have purpose. At this point, there are too many pieces for you to try to pick up. There are pieces missing. You couldn't put this back together even if you wanted to. You don't have time. Stop wasting time.

Let people think what they're going to think. You can't control their thoughts, but you can prove those thoughts wrong. Somebody will always have something to say about you. Negative or positive, they will have something to say. Lie or truth, they will have something to say. Don't waste time trying to explain *you*! No, let time do the telling. Even if you tried to explain *you* "they" still won't understand *you*. Prove them wrong by acting right!

Laugh at this. Keep doing what you're supposed to be doing. Keep becoming the new and better you! For now, forget about those pieces, or turn them into something you can use. Make it a project – a work of art. Use that heartbreak in a song. You don't have to run away from this. Instead of trying to put things back together, clean up. Clean up those emotions. Yes, make them useful.

Sometimes things are broken in order to make something more beautiful, like decoupage or glass mosaic. You can design this beautifully under your feet, my love, and walk all over it.

For a time, you might feel stuck – afraid to move – afraid of cutting yourself on that which is broken. My love, movement is worth it. Besides, time heals all wounds. However, if you stay stuck, you'll continue to suffer.

Find out how others did what you need to do, and do it. Don't let this stress you out! Don't let this drain you of your energy, little dove. No, just organize the pieces so you can walk all over them. When you create from this, you'll reap the benefits long after this is over. Be confident! You have what it takes! Yes, it may get lonely. Yes, it may be hard work. Do it anyway! My friend, *this* is going to help you get *that*.

Use This to Make That

"Life is not about waiting for the storms to pass…it's about learning how to dance in the rain."

~Vivian Greene

Situational Awareness

Use this exercise to examine five current situations you'd like to change

Note:

Sometimes it isn't possible to change a situation – some things are out of our control. When we can't change a situation, we should surrender to change and let change happen. We can help relieve some of the stress of the change by changing our perspective, having a positive attitude, letting go of the past, learning healthy ways to cope, trashing expired goals and/or expectations, and seeing its purpose or meaning.

S1. _____

Will S1 matter a year from now? **Yes/No**

Can *you* change S1? **Yes/No**

How do you want S1 to change?

_____
_____
_____
_____
_____
_____

What's your plan for change?

_____
_____
_____
_____
_____
_____

S2. _____

Will S2 matter a year from now? **Yes/No**

Can *you* change S2? **Yes/No**

How do you want S2 to change?

_____
_____
_____
_____
_____

What's your plan for change?

_____
_____
_____
_____
_____

S3. _____

Will S3 matter a year from now? **Yes/No**

Can *you* change S3? **Yes/No**

How do you want S3 to change?

_____
_____
_____
_____
_____

What's your plan for change?

_____
_____
_____
_____

S4. _____

Will S4 matter a year from now? **Yes/No**

Can *you* change S4? **Yes/No**

How do you want S4 to change?

_____
_____
_____
_____
_____

S5. _____

Will S5 matter a year from now? **Yes/No**

Can *you* change S5? **Yes/No**

How do you want S5 to change?

_____
_____
_____
_____
_____

What do you need to accept?

_____
_____
_____
_____
_____
_____
_____

What have you learned from your situations?

_____
_____
_____
_____
_____
_____
_____
_____
_____
_____
_____
_____
_____
_____
_____
_____
_____
_____
_____
_____
_____
_____
_____
_____
_____
_____

Can you use what you've learned to help someone else? **Yes/No**

Date of Change

S1: _____ Reward _____

S2: _____ Reward _____

S3: _____ Reward _____

S4: _____ Reward _____

S5: _____ Reward _____

Mon	Tue	Wed	Thr	Fri	Sat	Sun	Date: _____
○	○	○	○	○	○	○	

My goal(s):

My obstacle(s):

Plan to overcome obstacle(s):

Task to overcome each obstacle:

My hopes for the future:

Visualization (I see myself there already)

It looks like

It feels like

I see

I hear

Consistant with my dreams? **Yes/No**

Resources needed:

Skills I have that will help me accomplish my goal:

Positive affirmation:

My past failures resulted from
_____

Because
_____

Lesson learned
_____

Things to remember:

I will
_____

I will not
_____

I want
_____

I don't want
_____

I am
_____

I am not
_____

Because
_____

I will reward myself:

I _____ am commiting to myself this day of _____ year _____ to do the best I can possibly do while being the best I can possibly be in order to achieve my goal. I **WILL** reach my goal by _____, after which I will reward myself with the above for a job well done.

Signature_____ Witness_____

Results:

( ) Reward claimed   Date claimed

DAY 13
Time to Upgrade

You may not have noticed this, but every time you lose something, you gain something. Sometimes we lose something in order to be blessed with not necessarily something better but, rather, something needed.

I'll often give to others before I give to myself. I once walked around with a broken phone for months. It took me losing my purse in order to replace it. Well, now I have a new phone. This phone is better than the phone I had before. Sure, I lost all my contacts, but this is also a part of the setup. He said, "Where I am taking you, 'they' cannot come."

I'd been told this many times before, but I just wouldn't listen. I just couldn't do it. I felt as though I were giving up on people. I felt as though I were judging others for their choice of lifestyle. I'm no better than anyone else.

It is not about being better than anyone; it's about not going in the same direction as "everyone." It's about being set apart in order to truly listen and learn. If I can't learn to better myself from you, then I don't need to be around you. This is why we have to upgrade. We can't keep everything and everybody. We have to let some things go. Especially if they are outdated. Especially if they are no longer good for us. Especially if they become toxic.

Relationships end because they're outdated. It's time to upgrade. You got evicted because it's time for an upgrade. You can't keep living like that. You got sick because the Great Spirit wants to teach you how to take care of you better. It's time to upgrade you! All is well, my friend. You lose to gain.

When my baby passed away, I was almost done with God and life. I was. I was done! Until I remembered the dream I had before the events took place. This little girl saved me from a deep depression. This little girl who lived but for an hour did more for me than any doctor could and ever would. In this dream, she stood between me and my enemies and burst into a white light. She destroyed them! She saved me! She was God's gift of hope to me. So, you see, there's nothing to be sad about. She's not gone. No. We're just fighting the same war in different fields.

My friend, it might look like a loss right now, but just wait for it. You're about to gain. You are about to be blessed beyond what you can see! The Great Spirit is about to upgrade you. This next man coming into your life is going to be your keeper. He is going to make it known that you have his heart. Don't be afraid when things begin to move fast. This is a part of the upgrade. No worries. No tears. "They" had to go...in order for you to upgrade. All is well, my love. Yes, all is well.

You Will Lose to Gain

Note to Self:

"Because this exact leaf had to grow in that exact way, in that exact place, so that precise wind could tear it from that precise branch and make it fly into this exact face at that exact moment. And, if just one of those tiny little things had never had happened, I'd never have met ya. Which makes this leaf the most important leaf in human history."

~Neil Cross

Inventory

Take an inventory of your losses and gains (without using the word *nothing*).

What did you lose?	What did you gain?
What did you lose?	What did you gain?
What did you lose?	What did you gain?
What did you lose?	What did you gain?
What did you lose?	What did you gain?
What did you lose?	What did you gain?
What did you lose?	What did you gain?
What did you lose?	What did you gain?
What did you lose?	What did you gain?
What did you lose?	What did you gain?
What did you lose?	What did you gain?

What did you lose?	What did you gain?
What did you lose?	What did you gain?
What did you lose?	What did you gain?
What did you lose?	What did you gain?
What did you lose?	What did you gain?
What did you lose?	What did you gain?
What did you lose?	What did you gain?
What did you lose?	What did you gain?
What did you lose?	What did you gain?
What did you lose?	What did you gain?
What did you lose?	What did you gain?
What did you lose?	What did you gain?
What did you lose?	What did you gain?
What did you lose?	What did you gain?

| **Mon** | **Tue** | **Wed** | **Thr** | **Fri** | **Sat** | **Sun** | Date: _____ |
| O | O | O | O | O | O | O | |

My goal(s):

My obstacle(s):

Plan to overcome obstacle(s):

Task to overcome each obstacle:

My hopes for the future:

Visualization (I see myself there already)

It looks like

It feels like

I see

I hear

Consistant with my dreams? **Yes/No**

Resources needed:

Skills I have that will help me accomplish my goal:

Positive affirmation: _____

My past failures resulted from _____
_____

Because _____

Lesson learned _____

Things to remember: _____

I will _____

I will not _____

I want _____

I don't want _____

I am _____

I am not _____

Because _____

I will reward myself: _____

I _____ am commiting to myself this day of _____ year _____ to do the best I can possibly do while being the best I can possibly be in order to achieve my goal. I **WILL** reach my goal by _____, after which I will reward myself with the above for a job well done.

Signature_____ Witness_____

Results:

( ) Reward claimed   Date claimed

DAY 14
Take Responsibility

Don't be ashamed to admit your wrongs. You're human. This can be expected. You're learning. You're filled with emotions you don't have a manual for.

When buttons are pressed, you don't know what to expect. You're caught off guard. You don't know how to respond until you make the right response. You can't possibly know the right response – until you've made a few wrong ones.

Someone has pressed your buttons my love, but you're still responsible for your response. You decide if you want to act, react, or do nothing at all. You've made the choice to react. You panicked. Your ego felt endangered. It screamed at the top of its lungs to get your attention. That wasn't enough. It had to go running its mouth off to Pride. What did it do that for?

Pride doesn't listen. Pride argues with Truth – his own mother. He is a fool blinded by his own cause – you can't reason with a fool. Even if proven wrong, he'll try to win his case. Stay away from him, my love, "Pride goeth before destruction, and an haughty spirit before a fall."

No. Admit your wrongs. Take responsibility for your actions. Apologize and move on from this. Make a note about that button. Learn how to use it the correct way. I know you're angry. Just remember, "Anger is only one letter short of danger." Control your emotions. Don't let your emotions control you.

It's not a sin to be angry; it's only wise not to be. This isn't a sign of weakness. It's a sign of strength. It's a sign that you can hold up against pressure – like a person of steel. My friend, "Steel loses much of its value when it loses its temper." You and I both know this is going nowhere – especially not to a good place. You're not going to convince them – and they're not going to convince you. Calm yourself. Take a walk on middle ground. Allow time the time to tell.

Actions Cause Reactions

Note to Self:
_____
_____
_____
_____
_____
_____
_____

"When anger rises, think of the consequences."

~Confucius

Taking Responsibility?

Use the exercise below to see if you're taking responsibility for your own actions.

1. Do you know who you are?

    Yes ( )   No ( )   Sometimes ( )

    Who are you?

    _____
    _____
    _____
    _____
    _____
    _____
    _____
    _____
    _____
    _____
    _____
    _____

2. Do you know who you want to be?

    Yes ( )   No ( )   Sometimes ( )

    Who do you want to be?

    _____
    _____
    _____
    _____
    _____
    _____
    _____
    _____
    _____
    _____
    _____
    _____

3. Do you know what you want?

   Yes ( )   No ( )   Sometimes ( )

   What do you want?

   _____
   _____
   _____
   _____
   _____
   _____
   _____
   _____
   _____
   _____
   _____
   _____
   _____
   _____
   _____
   _____
   _____
   _____

4. Do you refrain from blaming others?

   Yes ( )   No ( )   Sometimes ( )

   If not, what do you often blame others for?

   _____
   _____
   _____
   _____
   _____
   _____
   _____
   _____
   _____
   _____
   _____
   _____
   _____
   _____
   _____

5. Are you honest with yourself?

   Yes ( )   No ( )   Sometimes ( )

   If not, what do you often lie to yourself about?

   _____
   _____
   _____
   _____
   _____
   _____
   _____
   _____
   _____
   _____

6. Do you find ways to benefit from negative things that happen in life?

   Yes ( )   No ( )   Sometimes ( )

   Why?

   _____
   _____
   _____
   _____
   _____
   _____

7. Can you control your emotions?

   Yes ( )   No ( )   Sometimes ( )

   Which emotions are difficult for you to control?

   _____
   _____
   _____
   _____
   _____
   _____
   _____
   _____

8. Do you often admit when you're "wrong" about something?

   Yes ( )   No ( )   Sometimes ( )

   What are you continuously "wrong" about?

   _____
   _____
   _____
   _____
   _____
   _____
   _____

9. Do you believe it's okay to make mistakes?

   Yes ( )   No ( )   Sometimes ( )

   What is your reasoning behind this belief?

   _____
   _____
   _____
   _____
   _____

10. Do you try not to feel sorry for yourself?

    Yes ( )   No ( )   Sometimes ( )

    If not, what do you often feel sorry for?

    _____
    _____
    _____
    _____

11. Do you often try to find ways to improve yourself?

    Yes ( )   No ( )   Sometimes ( )

    What are you currently trying to improve?

    _____
    _____
    _____
    _____
    _____
    _____
    _____

12. Do you consider yourself to be selfless?

    Yes ( )　　　　No ( )　　　　Sometimes ( )

    Describe your last selfless act:

    _____

13. Do you refrain from playing the role of a victim?

    Yes ( )　　　　No ( )　　　　Sometimes ( )

    Describe your last selfless act:

    _____

Calculate your score

How many "yes" answers do you have? _____

0 to 1: You don't take responsibility for your own actions. You're likely to be toxic to yourself and others. It would benefit you to soul search and self-evaluate.

1 to 4: You've tried to take responsibility for your own actions. However, your comfort causes conflict. People who score between one and four tend to be spoiled. There are likely people in your life who are enabling you to not do what you need to do for you. It would benefit you to start doing more for yourself.

4 to 8: You take responsibility for your actions when it's most beneficial for you to do so. Your mood often fluctuates, which is why you have no set emotional style. As a result, you're likely to *act, react, or do nothing at all* depending on your energy level or mental state. It would benefit you to find out what makes you happy, get creative, and socialize with positive people who love and respect you.

9 to 12: You're more likely to take responsibility for your own actions. However, there are times when you get caught up in the moment. It would benefit you to practice persistence.

12 to 13: You take full responsibility for your own actions. You've come a long way, my friend. Give yourself a pat on the back and don't forget to reward yourself for a job well done.

Mon	**Tue**	**Wed**	**Thr**	**Fri**	**Sat**	**Sun**	Date: _____
○	○	○	○	○	○	○	

My goal(s):

My obstacle(s):

Plan to overcome obstacle(s):

Task to overcome each obstacle:

My hopes for the future:

Visualization (I see myself there already)

It looks like
_____

It feels like
_____

I see
_____

I hear
_____

Consistant with my dreams? **Yes/No**

Resources needed:

Skills I have that will help me accomplish my goal:

Positive affirmation:

My past failures resulted from
_____

Because
_____

Lesson learned
_____

Things to remember:

I will
_____

I will not
_____

I want
_____

I don't want
_____

I am
_____

I am not
_____

Because
_____

I will reward myself:

I _____ am commiting to myself this day of _____ year _____ to do the best I can possibly do while being the best I can possibly be in order to achieve my goal. I **WILL** reach my goal by _____, after which I will reward myself with the above for a job well done.

Signature_____ Witness_____

Results:

( ) Reward claimed   Date claimed

DAY 15
Be Honest with Self

You're playing it safe. The life you're living right now is not truly the life you want. The way things are functioning around you is not what you desire. Maybe you're afraid to try. Maybe you're afraid to fail. My friend, the only way you fail is to not try. Ever hear the saying "You get an A for effort?" Get out of the GESOM! Get out of the "good enough" state of mind.

Circumstance will often teach us that we need to settle for good enough. No, I don't want to settle for good enough. Good enough just won't do. Good enough means you're just barely getting by. You're just going through the motions. You're settling for a D minus and not even trying to get an A.

Where I'm from, to some, good enough is success. Good enough is making it. Moving to the next town over is arriving at your destination. I can only imagine what it's like in the slums. I imagine their good enough is finding edible food and clean water. No, that just won't do. There's a difference between being good enough and settling for good enough.

We don't have to live in good enough. We don't have to settle for good enough. No, my friend, you deserve to be happy – and happy does not mean content. You deserve to be happy – and happy doesn't mean settling for less than you're worth.

Maybe you didn't grow up in the best of situations. Maybe you didn't have a fair start. Maybe you didn't have parents to raise, nurture, and teach you how to survive in a world full of greedy people; because, they didn't have parents to raise, nurture, and teach them. Who is going to break the cycle? Someone has to break the cycle.

My spirit spoke to me. It said, "Find the one thing you're good at and learn how to be great at it." Not by man's standards – by God's standards. A man is subject to jealousy. His word can never be surely trusted, but God's word, my friend, count on it.

Live the life you truly need to live! Consider the possibility that the dysfunction in your life is wreaking havoc, affecting your focus, decision making, behavior, and overall well-being. At some point, you're going to need to do something about this. You are your responsibility.

Things are going to shift and change for the better when you begin to change yourself, how you think, and what you do. Now, when you do this, be sure to keep your desired outcome in mind. You're gonna need to know your wants and needs – before you come face to face with sacrifice and temptation.

Some people aint gone like that you didn't ask them for permission to become the best you. Some people will try to get in your way, but run through and leap over. There's more for you, my love. Don't worry about "them." You see, you'll always know where to find "them." They'll still be in the same place. However, when you began to move, they won't be able to find you. Be encouraged on today. No matter where you are, you are on the right track. There's an opportunity coming. It's going to be the train to get you there. So, "Come along, my friend, come along. Get aboard and ride this train. Nothing on this train to lose – everything to gain."

Give Life Your Best

Note to Self:

_____
_____
_____
_____
_____
_____
_____
_____
_____
_____

"Never be bullied into silence. Never allow yourself to be made a victim. Accept no one's definition of your life; define yourself."

~Harvey Fierstein

Getting Uncomfortable

Are you willing to step out of your comfort zone? If so, read the statements below out loud.

I will face my fears.

I will not allow the fear of what people think or might think of me hold me back.

I will not be afraid to make a fool of myself.

I will not be afraid to stand out in the crowd.

I will embrace the uniqueness in me.

I will not be afraid to try new things.

I will accept that I'm less than perfect but always strive for perfection.

I will allow myself to live in the joy of a moment and not attach to an outcome.

I will not set myself up for frustration or disappointment.

I understand that I can't change people, certain places, or certain things, but I can control and change the way I act and react to them.

I will give the unknown a chance to teach me the things I need to know about it.

Add your personal statements:

_____
_____

_____
_____

_____
_____

_____
_____

_____
_____

Mon	Tue	Wed	Thr	Fri	Sat	Sun	Date: _____
○	○	○	○	○	○	○	

My goal(s):

My obstacle(s):

Plan to overcome obstacle(s):

Task to overcome each obstacle:

My hopes for the future:

Visualization (I see myself there already)

It looks like
_____
It feels like
_____
I see
_____
I hear
_____

Consistant with my dreams? **Yes/No**

Resources needed:

Skills I have that will help me accomplish my goal:

Positive affirmation:

My past failures resulted from
_____

Because
_____

Lesson learned
_____

Things to remember:

I will
_____

I will not
_____

I want
_____

I don't want
_____

I am
_____

I am not
_____

Because
_____

I will reward myself:

I _____ am commiting to myself this day of _____ year _____ to do the best I can possibly do while being the best I can possibly be in order to achieve my goal. I **WILL** reach my goal by _____, after which I will reward myself with the above for a job well done.

Signature_____ Witness_____

Results:

( ) Reward claimed   Date claimed

DAY 16
A Fresh Start

As you sit alone in silence, don't get discouraged. Don't be too hard on yourself. Things happen for a reason. I know you can't see it now. You've been blinded by distraction. You've been seduced by the temptation to give up on you. Time after time, you've given all of you away to others. What's left for you? My love, you have to save some you for you.

There are things you have to accomplish – a task to be completed. You have work to do. You need to be present. This is the time to get you back. This is the time to improve you. This is the time to become you. Take a seat in stability. Feel the courage to be. You're in transition to a fresh start.

You're a caterpillar in a cocoon. Soon, my friend, you'll be a butterfly in flight. People will be amazed by you. You'll have the opportunity to go places you couldn't go before. You'll be able to go higher. You'll be able to go further. No, you won't be limited or confined by circumstance. You're going to soar.

You've thought long enough. You've waited long enough. You've dreamed long enough. It's time to make those dreams a reality. It's time to take action. It's time to begin – again.

You may have to put a few people on hold. If they're true to you, they won't mind waiting. Don't keep wasting your time on people who don't add substance to your life. Don't miss out on the chance to improve your situation. Use silence to focus on you. Do something nice for you. Compliment yourself. Look in the mirror and start telling yourself how good you look.

Put more time into building you up. Give yourself some TLC. Tell you what you mean to you. You're good enough. Get back out there! You don't need them. You want them, but you don't need them.

Go do something fun, exciting, and new. It won't be as bad as you think. Get it out of your system. Realize you're human. It's natural to feel things. It's natural to desire. It's okay to want as long as you don't neglect your needs.

When you're done letting go, – when you're done crying about what doesn't matter; you're going to be able to focus on what matters. You're going to be able to embrace the silence. That ember is going to catch fire inside you. It's going to burn! You're going to be light to see light! As you sit there thinking about all the people who've let you down, how they're nowhere to be found when you "need" them, think about how you're keeping yourself down.

My love, you've been set apart for a reason. You have work to do. This is the best time to do it. Start now! You're equipped! You're enough! My friend, you have what it takes.

Don't Spoil Your Fresh Start

Note to Self:
_____
_____
_____
_____
_____
_____
_____
_____
_____
_____
_____
_____
_____
_____
_____
_____

"Nobody can go back and start a new beginning, but anyone can start today and make a new ending."

~Maria Robinson.

Starting Over

Fill in the blanks using only "Me," "Myself," and "I."

_____ know _____ can't start over in life while holding onto my past. I'm letting go of what's behind and embracing what is now to get to what is ahead. _____ will do my best to leave when _____ need to leave. _____ understand pain and suffering are not the same thing. _____ will not center my life around hurt, negativity, or failure. _____ accept what _____ cannot change to change what _____ can. _____ understand everything happens for a reason. _____ will do my best to remain alert and aware to identify the reasons. _____ will study to learn what I'm supposed to learn. _____ will not quit on my life. _____ will keep going even if _____ have to start over again and then again. _____ will stop asking others for permission to live. _____ will live, and _____ will live each day as if it were my last. _____ will be happy, _____ will be free, and _____ will be love. _____ will journey to discover my purpose. _____ know _____ don't know everything. _____ understand that I'm not expected to know everything. However, _____ will learn what _____ need to know to become. _____ will set goals, _____ will get organized, and _____ will at least try. _____ will take the time to get to know _____. _____ will take the time to plan. _____ will allow _____ to feel what _____ am feeling and learn how to deal with those feelings appropriately. _____ will determine exactly who it is _____ want to be. _____ will take care of _____. _____ will make an effort. _____ will not be negative. ____ will surround _____ with positive influences. ____ will be patient with _____. ____ will do my best to focus during the transition. ____ will make peace with the idea that life is a journey, not a destination. ____ will trust in my inner wisdom. ____ will not put _____ down. ____ will lift _____ up. ____ will just do what ____ need to do for _____. ____ will prepare _____. ____ will celebrate even the smallest of successes. ____ will mentally hoard what works. ____ won't be afraid to try new things. ____ will keep moving no matter what obstacles may stand in my way. ____ will not allow _____ to be discouraged by delay. ____ will allow _____ to enjoy the ride and have fun. ____ will focus on taking one step at a time.

____ will be _____.

Note to Self:

_____
_____
_____
_____
_____
_____
_____
_____
_____

Mon	Tue	Wed	Thr	Fri	Sat	Sun	Date: _____
○	○	○	○	○	○	○	

My goal(s):

My obstacle(s):

Plan to overcome obstacle(s):

Task to overcome each obstacle:

My hopes for the future:

Visualization (I see myself there already)

It looks like
_____

It feels like
_____

I see
_____

I hear
_____

Consistant with my dreams? **Yes/No**

Resources needed:

Skills I have that will help me accomplish my goal:

Positive affirmation:

My past failures resulted from
_____

Because
_____

Lesson learned
_____

Things to remember:

I will
_____

I will not
_____

I want
_____

I don't want
_____

I am
_____

I am not
_____

Because
_____

I will reward myself:

I _____ am commiting to myself this day of _____ year _____ to do the best I can possibly do while being the best I can possibly be in order to achieve my goal. I **WILL** reach my goal by _____, after which I will reward myself with the above for a job well done.

Signature_____ Witness_____

Results:

( ) Reward claimed   Date claimed

DAY 17
Get Power Back

Someone's hurt you. They've brainwashed you. They've tricked you into becoming someone other than you. You've lost yourself in the process. Sometimes you look in the mirror and don't recognize you. Sometimes you talk and don't hear you. Someone has taken something from you. Get it back!

Someone has stolen your power. They've drained you. You don't have energy left for you. No. Recharge! Get your power back! Plug into the source. Get turned on by the spirit.

You are not what they say you are. You're not weak. You've just been drained. Plug in. Focus on you. Take back your life! It doesn't belong to them! It's your life to live – and it is not over yet.

You have time to recharge. Get out of the "woe is me" state of mind. Do something about it! Start making necessary changes. Stop complaining. If you think you're fat, start working out. If you think you're lazy, go get a job. Clean up! Organize! Do something instead of complaining about everything!

My friend, be modest in your approach. You don't have to talk about it. You just need to be about it. "Actions speak louder than words."

Don't be afraid to ask for help. There's nothing wrong with wanting to better you. There is nothing wrong with wanting to be you again. You can become you again – better than before, actually. You can recharge, but be warned: modesty doesn't mean easy. You're going to have to make the effort. It's hard work, but my love, you're worth it. You have what it takes. You're equipped. You're enough. You are what you seek. Plug in.

It's important to be accurate in self-perception. You're not accurate about you at this moment. You've lost your identity. Take some time to get to know you again. Claim you. Then find your purpose. Claim your purpose. Then strive to become the better you.

My love, I know you're feeling tired right now, but get up. This is not your final resting place. Your battery is not completely dead. You have enough energy to get up. Now, get up. Go plug back in. Recharge!

Plug in and Recharge

"The most common way people give up their power
is by thinking they don't have any."

~Alice Walker

Get Your Power Back

Your power cord has been unplugged. Use this exercise to plug yourself back in. Fill in the blanks and then read the entire statement out loud.

I was unplugged from my source of power when I allowed _____.

I lost _____ as a result.

I felt _____.

It was difficult for me to _____
_____.

I no longer had enough _____ or
_____.

I was _____ and
_____.

I'd often tell myself, If only _____
_____,

I would be _____.

If only _____
_____,

my life would be _____.

If only _____
_____,

everything would be _____.

However, I understand I must trash my "if only" statements in order to focus on the *now*. I realize I don't need an outside source to plug into. The power is in me. I am the only person who has the power to charge my life. Therefore, I will no longer give my power away to others, but I will let my light shine upon them. I will reconnect to me and make choices for myself. I will identify limiting beliefs and core fears. When I am afraid, I will not let fear control me. I will express myself and let my faith reign. I will change

_____

_____

_____

_____

_____

_____

_____

_____

_____

_____

_____. I will tune into my inner self and not allow myself to be distracted by the outer noise. I will take responsibility for me. I understand I don't have the power to change all things, but I have the power to change me in relation to everything. I will observe my thoughts consistently, and cultivate self-worth and self-love. I will continue to move forward no matter the obstacle standing in my way. I will begin to trust me again. I will forgive and not hoard unforgiveness. I will start growing! I will start thriving! I will start living! I will plug back into the source of my power and start shining!

Mon	**Tue**	**Wed**	**Thr**	**Fri**	**Sat**	**Sun**	Date: _____
○	○	○	○	○	○	○	

My goal(s):

My obstacle(s):

Plan to overcome obstacle(s):

Task to overcome each obstacle:

My hopes for the future:

Visualization (I see myself there already)

It looks like
_____

It feels like
_____

I see
_____

I hear
_____

Consistant with my dreams? **Yes/No**

Resources needed:

Skills I have that will help me accomplish my goal:

Positive affirmation:

My past failures resulted from
_____

Because
_____

Lesson learned
_____

Things to remember:

I will
_____

I will not
_____

I want
_____

I don't want
_____

I am
_____

I am not
_____

Because
_____

I will reward myself:

I _____ am commiting to myself this day of _____ year _____ to do the best I can possibly do while being the best I can possibly be in order to achieve my goal. I **WILL** reach my goal by _____, after which I will reward myself with the above for a job well done.

Signature_____ Witness_____

Results:

( ) Reward claimed   Date claimed

DAY 18
Aware of Purpose

We exist for a reason: we have something to do. We're all on a mission. We all have assignments. You might not be assigned to the same task as others. That doesn't mean you don't have one. Everyone has something to do. It is when someone doesn't do what they're supposed to be doing that the scales tip off balance.

First, you must find your purpose to become. What's the reason you were born? Is it to invent? Is it to nurture? Is it to lead? Is it to follow? Or is it just to be? Until you figure this out, you will continue to be unhappy. You will continue to blame others for your shortcomings. You will continue to make the same "mistakes."

No, they're doing what they're assigned to do. Find out what you're supposed to be doing and do it. You have to feed the hen in order to get the egg, my love. Do your part. Learn from the ants. Look around to see the perfect order of things. My friend, you fit in somewhere.

Don't be afraid to take action. Don't be afraid to make strides towards your goals. There are good things to come once you start moving in your life. You'll see new things. You'll meet new people. You'll be healed. And you will prosper.

You can clear the path to success only when you know your purpose. If what you do is not in line with what you're supposed to be doing, you will not succeed at it. Yes, you will fail. Not as a person. You will fail that assignment, because it is the wrong assignment.

When you're walking according to your purpose, there's not a demon or devil in "hell" that can stop you. There's not a man on earth that can take it from you. It is your birthright. Your destiny belongs to you.

No one is going to do this for you, my love. They can't save you. Save yourself! Start working on you. Find your purpose and become who it is you're destined to become. Don't be afraid to step into you. Don't be afraid to dream – and don't be afraid to wake up from your dreams to make them reality.

Little dove, if you continue to look for it, you will find your song and you'll sing it beautifully. I see what you don't see. Believe me, my love; others will rise the moment you choose to make a sound in this world.

Find Your Purpose

Note to Self:

"The two most important days in your life are the day you're born and the day you discover why."

~Mark Twain

Finding Purpose

Set aside some time for quiet contemplation with a pen and an empty note book to answer the questions below. No worries. There aren't any right or wrong answers – be open and completely honest with yourself.

1. Are you ready to find your life purpose?
2. What's your life philosophy?
3. When you were a child, what did you love to do?
4. Do you feel there's a part of you that still loves the things you loved as a child?
5. What do you miss most about your childhood?
6. What moments do you remember best from your past?
7. What do you often daydream about?
8. If you could be whoever you wanted to be, who would you choose to be?
9. If you could do whatever you wanted, what would you choose to do?
10. What sorts of things fascinate you?
11. What makes you feel great about yourself?
12. Who do you admire?
13. Who inspires you most?
14. Who reminds you of you?
15. What sensory experiences do you remember best?
16. What are your talents?
17. What makes you smile?
18. Who are you?
19. Who do you think you are?

20. Who do you want to be?
21. How would you describe yourself to a stranger?
22. What are the most important characteristics that define your identity?
23. What are your top 50 goals from highest priority to least?
24. What activities make you lose track of time?
25. What qualities or habits would you like to develop?
26. What are the top 100 things you like to do in order of importance?
27. What's the one big dream you would have pursued if everything had gone your way?
28. What are 10 words that describe you?
29. What do you want to change about your life?
30. What would you do with all the money in the world?
31. What is the one thing you want to experience or accomplish before you die?
32. What would you do if you only had a day left to live?
33. What would you regret not fully doing, being, or having in your life?
34. What were some challenges, difficulties, and hardships you've overcome or are in the process of overcoming? How did you do it?
35. What have you conquered and need to share to make the world a better place?
36. What are the things you would do even if you didn't get paid for it?
37. If you had to teach something, what would you teach?

38. What do other people say you're really good at, or that you should do professionally, or do more of?
39. What do people typically ask you for help in?
40. What are you naturally good at?
41. What are you doing now?
42. What do you want to do?
43. Are you happy? Make a list of times you've been happiest in life. What were you doing? Who were you with? Do you still manage to find time to engage in these activities? Why?
44. What's most important to you?
45. If you could get a message across to a large group of people, who would those people be? What would your message be?
46. What would your perfect day look like? Describe every detail.
47. How does the perfect day bring out the best in you?
48. What are your core values?
49. What causes do you strongly believe in? Connect with?
50. What's your personality type?
51. Who is your ideal self?
52. What 100 things are you scared to do?
53. What gives you a sense of purpose?
54. What do you hope your purpose in life is?
55. What is your life purpose?

Great Job! Now use only the answers to the questions in this exercise to create your personal mission statement. Write your mission statement in the space below when finished.

Mon	Tue	Wed	Thr	Fri	Sat	Sun	Date: _____
○	○	○	○	○	○	○	

My goal(s):

My obstacle(s):

Plan to overcome obstacle(s):

Task to overcome each obstacle:

My hopes for the future:

Visualization (I see myself there already)

It looks like

It feels like

I see

I hear

Consistant with my dreams? **Yes/No**

Resources needed:

Skills I have that will help me accomplish my goal:

Positive affirmation:

My past failures resulted from
_____

Because
_____

Lesson learned
_____

Things to remember:

I will
_____

I will not
_____

I want
_____

I don't want
_____

I am
_____

I am not
_____

Because
_____

I will reward myself:

I _____ am commiting to myself this day of _____ year _____ to do the best I can possibly do while being the best I can possibly be in order to achieve my goal. I **WILL** reach my goal by _____, after which I will reward myself with the above for a job well done.

Signature_____ Witness_____

Results:

( ) Reward claimed   Date claimed

DAY 19
Learn from Nature

In this case, you either jump with the possibility of survival, or stay stuck and starve to death. This is what I've learned from a family of geese nesting on a tower of rocks. The parents hoped to keep their young safe. However, they knew the time would come when they'd have to leave the nest. They'd all have to do the unthinkable – jump off the tower to go find food.

First, the father jumped. Then the mother. The chicks were confused. How in the world were they going to get way down there? They couldn't fly.

The mother beckoned for them to join her. The first chick was hesitant, but instinct told him to jump, so he did. He jumped and hit his head on rock after rock while free-falling to the ground.

The second chick thought, "Well, if the first chick did it, why the heck not." He jumped off the tower, hitting his head on rock after rock while free-falling to the ground. The third chick jumped in the same like manner, but he jumped down the wrong side of the tower and was lost.

The fourth chick slipped. He wasn't even trying to jump. Oh no! He hit his head on rock after rock while free-falling to the ground. However, this chick landed in the perfect place.

Finally, it was down to the last chick. He'd watched all the other chicks, and now it was his turn. He made the perfect launch in confidence. It was all good. He soared. Until he ended up hitting his head on some rocks while free-falling to the ground.

When it was all said and done, one chick didn't make it, one chick was lost, one chick made the perfect landing, one chick was in a bad way, and one chick was slow to catch up.

Five jumped, but, only three made it through. If they hadn't jumped, all of them would have eventually died on that tower of rocks. They would have died in a hard place to live.

My friend, you've had a rough start. You've slipped and hit your head on some rocks. Be of good cheer, my love; you're going to land in the perfect place.

My friend, you've willingly sacrificed, but ended up hurting yourself in the end. Be of good cheer; you may be slow to catch up, but you'll move past this to lead the others.

Little dove, you made the perfect launch, but you're hurt badly. Get up and shake it off. It hurts, but you can move past this.

For the one lost, I pray you find yourself. And for the one that didn't make it, may your soul rest in peace.

You Will Land Accordingly

Note to Self:

"Learn character from trees, values from roots, and change from leaves."

~Tasneem Hameed

Should you do it?

List eight activities you've been contemplating participating in and do a potential risk assessment for each one.

1. _____

Positive	Good	Bad	Crippling	Damaging	Hindering	Negative
○	○	○	○	○	○	○

Conscious	Not Conscious	Productive	Unproductive	Occupational
○	○	○	○	○

Free	Cost Money	Alone	With Others	Planned	Spontanious
○	○	○	○	○	○

Physical	Mental	Emotional	Social	Sexual	Last time?
○	○	○	○	○	_____

What do you hope to get out of participating in this activity?
_____

Is it going to affect your health or well-being? **Yes/No**

Are you going to do it? **Yes/No**

2. _____

Positive	Good	Bad	Crippling	Damaging	Hindering	Negative
○	○	○	○	○	○	○

Conscious	Not Conscious	Productive	Unproductive	Occupational
○	○	○	○	○

Free	Cost Money	Alone	With Others	Planned	Spontanious
○	○	○	○	○	○

Physical	Mental	Emotional	Social	Sexual	Last time?
○	○	○	○	○	_____

What do you hope to get out of participating in this activity?
_____

Is it going to affect your health or well-being? **Yes/No**

Are you going to do it? **Yes/No**

3. _____

Positive   Good   Bad   Crippling   Damaging   Hindering   Negative
   ○   ○   ○   ○   ○   ○   ○
Conscious   Not Conscious   Productive   Unproductive   Occupational
   ○   ○   ○   ○   ○
Free   Cost Money   Alone   With Others   Planned   Spontanious
 ○   ○   ○   ○   ○   ○
Physical   Mental   Emotional   Social   Sexual   Last time?
   ○   ○   ○   ○   ○   _____

What do you hope to get out of participating in this activity?
_____

Is it going to affect your health or well-being? **Yes/No**

Are you going to do it? **Yes/No**

4. _____

Positive   Good   Bad   Crippling   Damaging   Hindering   Negative
   ○   ○   ○   ○   ○   ○   ○
Conscious   Not Conscious   Productive   Unproductive   Occupational
   ○   ○   ○   ○   ○
Free   Cost Money   Alone   With Others   Planned   Spontanious
 ○   ○   ○   ○   ○   ○
Physical   Mental   Emotional   Social   Sexual   Last time?
   ○   ○   ○   ○   ○   _____

What do you hope to get out of participating in this activity?
_____

Is it going to affect your health or well-being? **Yes/No**

Are you going to do it? **Yes/No**

5. _____

Positive	Good	Bad	Crippling	Damaging	Hindering	Negative
○	○	○	○	○	○	○

Conscious	Not Conscious	Productive	Unproductive	Occupational
○	○	○	○	○

Free	Cost Money	Alone	With Others	Planned	Spontanious
○	○	○	○	○	○

Physical	Mental	Emotional	Social	Sexual	Last time?
○	○	○	○	○	_____

What do you hope to get out of participating in this activity?

_____

Is it going to affect your health or well-being? **Yes/No**

Are you going to do it? **Yes/No**

6. _____

Positive	Good	Bad	Crippling	Damaging	Hindering	Negative
○	○	○	○	○	○	○

Conscious	Not Conscious	Productive	Unproductive	Occupational
○	○	○	○	○

Free	Cost Money	Alone	With Others	Planned	Spontanious
○	○	○	○	○	○

Physical	Mental	Emotional	Social	Sexual	Last time?
○	○	○	○	○	_____

What do you hope to get out of participating in this activity?

_____

Is it going to affect your health or well-being? **Yes/No**

Are you going to do it? **Yes/No**

7. _____

Positive   Good   Bad   Crippling   Damaging   Hindering   Negative
   ○   ○   ○   ○   ○   ○   ○

Conscious   Not Conscious   Productive   Unproductive   Occupational
   ○   ○   ○   ○   ○

Free   Cost Money   Alone   With Others   Planned   Spontanious
 ○   ○   ○   ○   ○   ○

Physical   Mental   Emotional   Social   Sexual   Last time?
   ○   ○   ○   ○   ○   _____

What do you hope to get out of participating in this activity?

_____

Is it going to affect your health or well-being? **Yes/No**

Are you going to do it? **Yes/No**

8. _____

Positive   Good   Bad   Crippling   Damaging   Hindering   Negative
   ○   ○   ○   ○   ○   ○   ○

Conscious   Not Conscious   Productive   Unproductive   Occupational
   ○   ○   ○   ○   ○

Free   Cost Money   Alone   With Others   Planned   Spontanious
 ○   ○   ○   ○   ○   ○

Physical   Mental   Emotional   Social   Sexual   Last time?
   ○   ○   ○   ○   ○   _____

What do you hope to get out of participating in this activity?

_____

Is it going to affect your health or well-being? **Yes/No**

Are you going to do it? **Yes/No**

Mon	**Tue**	**Wed**	**Thr**	**Fri**	**Sat**	**Sun**	Date: _____
○	○	○	○	○	○	○	

My goal(s):

My obstacle(s):

Plan to overcome obstacle(s):

Task to overcome each obstacle:

My hopes for the future:

Visualization (I see myself there already)

It looks like
_____
It feels like
_____
I see
_____
I hear
_____
Consistant with my dreams? **Yes/No**

Resources needed:

Skills I have that will help me accomplish my goal:

Positive affirmation:

My past failures resulted from
_____

Because
_____

Lesson learned
_____

Things to remember:

I will
_____

I will not
_____

I want
_____

I don't want
_____

I am
_____

I am not
_____

Because
_____

I will reward myself:

I _____ am commiting to myself this day of _____ year _____ to do the best I can possibly do while being the best I can possibly be in order to achieve my goal. I **WILL** reach my goal by _____, after which I will reward myself with the above for a job well done.

Signature_____ Witness_____

Results:

( ) Reward claimed   Date claimed

DAY 20
Invent the New You

You may have heard that "things don't happen overnight." However, something does happen when it's dark. It's called growth. Growth doesn't stop until life ends. Sometimes not even death can stop growth.

My friend, it might be dark in your life, but you're making progress. Every day, you're growing more and more. You're becoming more and more. It is sufficient for the moment.

You can't be perfect until you have all that's required for perfection. Even after you become the beautiful flower, you still may have a few thorns at your side. You still might grow beside some weeds. The wind may cause you to lose a few petals. Without taking precautions, you could still be infested by pests and become diseased. Guess what? You still bless the world with your beauty.

You don't have to wait till you become in order to do this. You can start now by just being – by being present in this moment. The fact that you're even thinking about this right now speaks volumes. You will better yourself because you want to better yourself.

An invention begins with a thought. You are thinking about inventing a new and improved you. I'm not going to lie to you, my friend; it's going to be some work. You have a few wrong ingredients. You have unforgiveness. Bitterness. You have fear. You have doubt. You have addiction. You have anxiety – along with other things. This isn't helping you to invent you. It is destroying you. It's giving you a bad taste.

Make a commitment to you. Put together a plan to better you. Then, after you have the plan, take action. If you do this, my love, you will invent a new you that's not only good looking; you will invent a you that will be useful – to you as well as others.

Invent the Better You

Note to Self:

___
___
___
___
___
___
___

"The reinvention of daily life means marching of the edge of our maps."

~Bob Black

Invent the New You

The child in you is crawling away from responsibility. Use the next page to help the child in you grow into the bigger, better you.

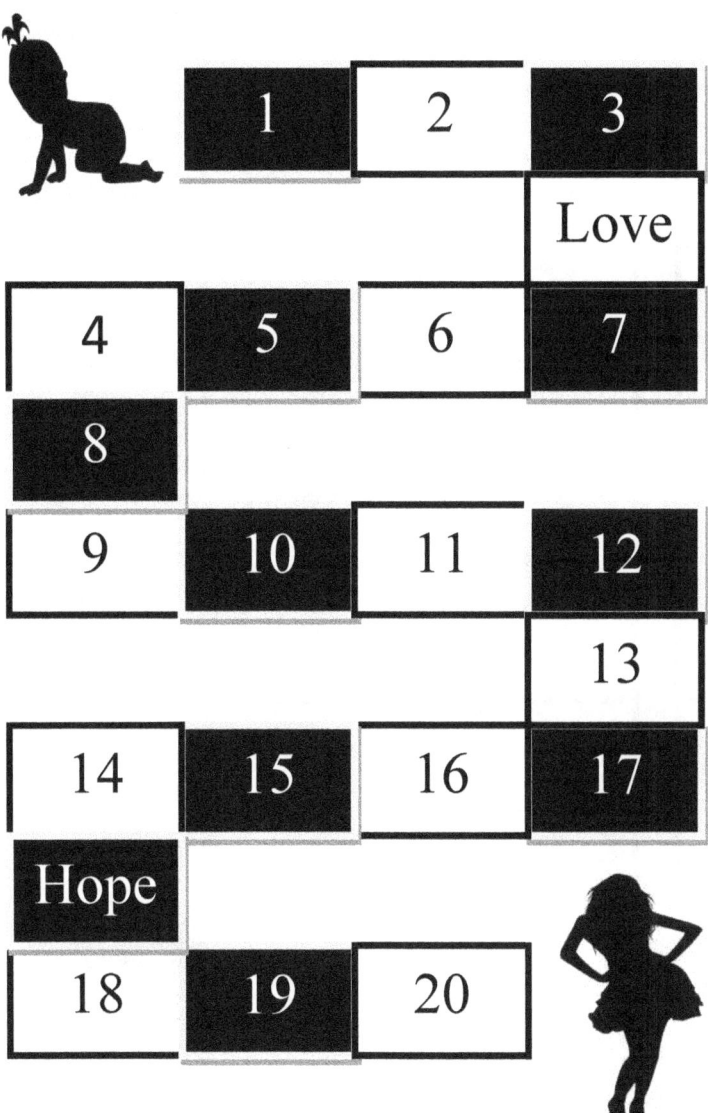

1 Visualize your new future	2 Write down changes you want to make	3 Write down changes you need to make	Love Practice self-love
4 Create a plan for making the changes	5 Write down some reasonable goals	6 Set a deadline to accomplish goals	7 Discover your purpose
8 Remind yourself of your vision	9 Journal daily for at least 10 minutes	10 Know why you want to reinvent yourself	11 Don't allow others to draw you into the old
12 Address your flaws	13 Improve the way you think	14 Improve the way you interact with others	15 Improve your health
16 Improve your education	17 Organize and purge the unnecessary	Hope Try to stay positive and motivated	18 Trash bad habits
19 Avoid distraction	20 Change the way you look	Become Be the best you can be	**Meet the new you!**

Mon	Tue	Wed	Thr	Fri	Sat	Sun	Date: _____
○	○	○	○	○	○	○	

My goal(s):

My obstacle(s):

Plan to overcome obstacle(s):

Task to overcome each obstacle:

My hopes for the future:

Visualization (I see myself there already)

It looks like
_____
It feels like
_____
I see
_____
I hear
_____
Consistant with my dreams? **Yes/No**

Resources needed:

Skills I have that will help me accomplish my goal:

Positive affirmation:

My past failures resulted from
_____

Because
_____

Lesson learned
_____

Things to remember:

I will
_____

I will not
_____

I want
_____

I don't want
_____

I am
_____

I am not
_____

Because
_____

I will reward myself:

I _____ am commiting to myself this day of _____ year _____ to do the best I can possibly do while being the best I can possibly be in order to achieve my goal. I **WILL** reach my goal by _____, after which I will reward myself with the above for a job well done.

Signature_____ Witness_____

Results:

( ) Reward claimed   Date claimed

DAY 21
Positive Change

My friend, peace begins at home. It's the birthplace of true prosperity. There is an old saying, "If there is righteousness in the heart, there will be beauty in the character. If there be beauty in the character, there will be harmony in the home. If there is harmony in the home, there will be order in the nation. When there is order in the nation, there will be peace in the world."

You see, my love, it all begins with you. You have the power to create positive change. You have the power to impact this world with what you contribute to it. In order to contribute, you have to make time for contribution. You don't have to do everything at once. It's been said, "Little and often make much." I truly believe this. Do what you can when you can.

You're entering into a season of wealth and abundance. Instead of planting millet, you've planted a tree. Now go plant men. Do not be selfish. Instead, be selfless. Use this harvest to help feed others. Fill your baskets with what's needed. Then share what's left. You can't consume it all – it will spoil.

You can only preserve this by putting it into something. I encourage you to put it in others. Do you understand?

You have the power to do great things. You have the power to do something that others can't or are unwilling to do. You have the power to give. You have the power to create positive change. It doesn't have to be money. It doesn't have to be food. It could simply be your time. You can teach others to get to where you're at. You can help lead children in the right direction. You can do something – which is better than doing nothing.

My friend, don't create waste. Don't hoard this blessing. Don't be a glutton. Share the wealth. An abundance of something is coming your way my love. Be wise in your dealings and watch how you play your cards. Remember to create positive change.

Make the Contribution

Note to Self:

_____
_____
_____
_____
_____
_____

"Do all the good you can, by all the means you can, in all the ways you can, in all the places you can, at all the times you can, for all the people you can, as long as ever you can."

~John Wesley

Changing the World

Make a list of things you can do to help create positive change in the world.

1. _____
   Date of Contribution: _____ Amount $_____
2. _____
   Date of Contribution: _____ Amount $_____
3. _____
   Date of Contribution: _____ Amount $_____
4. _____
   Date of Contribution: _____ Amount $_____
5. _____
   Date of Contribution: _____ Amount $_____
6. _____
   Date of Contribution: _____ Amount $_____
7. _____
   Date of Contribution: _____ Amount $_____
8. _____
   Date of Contribution: _____ Amount $_____
9. _____
   Date of Contribution: _____ Amount $_____
10. _____
    Date of Contribution: _____ Amount $_____
11. _____
    Date of Contribution: _____ Amount $_____
12. _____
    Date of Contribution: _____ Amount $_____

13. _____
    Date of Contribution: _____ Amount $_____
14. _____
    Date of Contribution: _____ Amount $_____
15. _____
    Date of Contribution: _____ Amount $_____
16. _____
    Date of Contribution: _____ Amount $_____
17. _____
    Date of Contribution: _____ Amount $_____
18. _____
    Date of Contribution: _____ Amount $_____
19. _____
    Date of Contribution: _____ Amount $_____
20. _____
    Date of Contribution: _____ Amount $_____
21. _____
    Date of Contribution: _____ Amount $_____
22. _____
    Date of Contribution: _____ Amount $_____
23. _____
    Date of Contribution: _____ Amount $_____
24. _____
    Date of Contribution: _____ Amount $_____
25. _____
    Date of Contribution: _____ Amount $_____
26. _____
    Date of Contribution: _____ Amount $_____
27. _____
    Date of Contribution: _____ Amount $_____

Mon	**Tue**	**Wed**	**Thr**	**Fri**	**Sat**	**Sun**	Date: _____
○	○	○	○	○	○	○	

My goal(s):

My obstacle(s):

Plan to overcome obstacle(s):

Task to overcome each obstacle:

My hopes for the future:

Visualization (I see myself there already)

It looks like
_____
It feels like
_____
I see
_____
I hear
_____
Consistant with my dreams? **Yes/No**

Resources needed:

Skills I have that will help me accomplish my goal:

Positive affirmation:

My past failures resulted from
_____

Because
_____

Lesson learned
_____

Things to remember:

I will
_____

I will not
_____

I want
_____

I don't want
_____

I am
_____

I am not
_____

Because
_____

I will reward myself:

I _____ am commiting to myself this day of _____ year _____ to do the best I can possibly do while being the best I can possibly be in order to achieve my goal. I **WILL** reach my goal by _____, after which I will reward myself with the above for a job well done.

Signature_____ Witness_____

Results:

( ) Reward claimed   Date claimed

DAY 22
Turn Dirt into Mud

Dirt can be a good thing, but it can also be a nuisance, especially when it's found in places where it's not wanted nor needed. Especially when it's just there to be there without purpose of being.

My friend, you can't really do much with dirt until you get it wet. You can't really do much with it except walk all over it until you add something to it. It's good if you're trying to fill in a hole in the ground. But get this: "Fill dirt is earthy material which is used to fill in a *depression* or hole in the ground or create *mounds* or otherwise *artificially change* the grade or *evaluation* of real property."

Yes. You may not have realized this, but dirt – the stuff you walk on every day – is a mixture of "stuff" that has been broken down over time. It is loose soil that no longer can support plant life. In other words, nothing that is good for you can grow in dirt until it becomes soil – it has to get wet first.

When dirt is dirt, it is just dirt. It is a nuisance. It is a circumstance that causes inconvenience and annoyance. It's filthy and unpleasant to look at. It is the stuff that stunts your growth. It is the stuff that can cause you to wilt and die.

Dirt is everywhere. You don't have to find it. It will find you. You don't have to ask for it. You don't have to pay for it. My friend, you can't just get rid of it! So turn it into something that you can use.

Get it wet! Add something to it. Throw in some straw, grass, or pine needles. Start making bricks out of your situation. Start building a shelter. Start laying a foundation to stand firmly on. My friend, you might just have to get your hands "dirty." You might have to be uncomfortable! You might even be faced with irritations.

It is not always going to be easy. It's definitely going to be some work, but guess what? If you put in the effort, you will get beautiful results. Your dirt will become valuable. Your dirt can become building material. Do you understand?

My friend, if you just add the right stuff, that dirt can become fertile soil to nourish and help you grow, beautiful flower. It would be better for you to rise like dust than to just sit there doing nothing – going nowhere. My friend, things will get better for you – when you begin to make them better for you.

Make It Work for You

"Some people want it to happen, some wish it would happen, others make it happen."

~Michael Jordan

Cleaning Up Your Life

At no point in time will every area of your life be perfect. However, it's still your responsibility to live and be as clean, useful, healthy, happy, and balanced as possible. Take a look at the areas of life listed below. Which areas are clean? Which areas require more attention than others? Which areas are in between – or just there?

1. **Career**

    Clean ( )　　Unclean ( )　　Neither ( )

2. **Community**

    Clean ( )　　Unclean ( )　　Neither ( )

3. **Education**

    Clean ( )　　Unclean ( )　　Neither ( )

4. **Emotional State**

    Clean ( )　　Unclean ( )　　Neither ( )

5. **Environment**

    Clean ( )　　Unclean ( )　　Neither ( )

6. **Family**

    Clean ( )　　Unclean ( )　　Neither ( )

7. **Finance**

    Clean ( )　　Unclean ( )　　Neither ( )

8. **Fitness**

    Clean ( )　　Unclean ( )　　Neither ( )

9. **Fun**

    Clean ( )　　Unclean ( )　　Neither ( )

10. **Health**

    Clean ( )　　Unclean ( )　　Neither ( )

11. **Home**

                Clean ( )   Unclean ( )   Neither ( )

12. **Intimacy**

                Clean ( )   Unclean ( )   Neither ( )

13. **Legal**

                Clean ( )   Unclean ( )   Neither ( )

14. **Love**

                Clean ( )   Unclean ( )   Neither ( )

15. **Mental State**

                Clean ( )   Unclean ( )   Neither ( )

16. **Physical**

                Clean ( )   Unclean ( )   Neither ( )

17. **Purpose**

                Clean ( )   Unclean ( )   Neither ( )

18. **Relationship**

                Clean ( )   Unclean ( )   Neither ( )

19. **Self-knowledge**

                Clean ( )   Unclean ( )   Neither ( )

20. **Social**

                Clean ( )   Unclean ( )   Neither ( )

21. **Spiritual**

                Clean ( )   Unclean ( )   Neither ( )

Note to Self:

_____
_____
_____
_____
_____
_____
_____

Mon	Tue	Wed	Thr	Fri	Sat	Sun	Date: _____
○	○	○	○	○	○	○	

My goal(s):

My obstacle(s):

Plan to overcome obstacle(s):

Task to overcome each obstacle:

My hopes for the future:

Visualization (I see myself there already)

It looks like
_____

It feels like
_____

I see
_____

I hear
_____

Consistant with my dreams? **Yes/No**

Resources needed:

Skills I have that will help me accomplish my goal:

Positive affirmation:

My past failures resulted from
_____

Because
_____

Lesson learned
_____

Things to remember:

I will
_____

I will not
_____

I want
_____

I don't want
_____

I am
_____

I am not
_____

Because
_____

I will reward myself:

I _____ am commiting to myself this day of _____ year _____ to do the best I can possibly do while being the best I can possibly be in order to achieve my goal. I **WILL** reach my goal by _____, after which I will reward myself with the above for a job well done.

Signature_____ Witness_____

Results:

( ) Reward claimed   Date claimed

DAY 23
Stand Up

There are people in this world sitting down. Stand up! Come out of your comfort zone. Get to work in your life. I know it's scary. I know it's hard work, but it's also necessary work. You'll have to do this before you get that.

Stop depending on others to do this for you. They won't do it! They can't do it! This isn't part of their assignment. They don't have the tools. They're not equipped with what you've been equipped with. You have what it takes!

I need you to start believing you're enough. You were born enough! It's hurtful. Trust me, I know. You do everything for everybody, but when it's time for them to show up for you, they don't even bother. They flake and make up excuses. No worries. I'll tell you this again: you don't need them to help you with this.

You don't need their support! They were not put on this earth to help you! You were put here to help them. You have the support of the Great Spirit, little dove. That's all you need. With His support, you have the POWER to speak things into existence. You have the POWER to change lives by just being.

It's okay to be you. You don't have to hide. Stand up! Start walking into your destiny. Don't complain about what others are doing. You're still sitting down. Stand up!

People don't understand you. Stand up! You're still believing what that person told you years ago. My friend, it's a LIE! Stand up! The doctor gave you a bad report. He said you'll NEVER... My friend, you're still here. Stand up!

Have faith and believe it's possible. Stand up! You have work to do. You're destined for greatness. Come out of comfort and contentment. Get out of your "woe is me" state of mind. Stand up!

Light, shine for all men to see. Don't wait. Do it now! Do it right now! Time is not going to stop for you, my friend. Stop wasting time! What's today will be tomorrow if you don't do something about it.

Yes, start living, my love. Stand up! Start walking! Get to work in your life! Stop letting your past control your future. Stop imagining your failure. There's more ahead for you, my love. Your greater is ahead! The life you want, need, and deserve is ahead! Stand up! Stand up, my love. Start walking. Go take back what belongs to you. It's your life.

You Can Do It

"Stand up and walk out of your history."

~Dr. Phil McGraw

220 / 31 DAYS WITH SHAN

Who said that?

Who made the following statements?

Mark Twain, Lao Tzu, T.S. Eliot, Oprah Winfrey, Tony Robbins, Albert Einstein, Donald Trump, André Gide, Steve Jobs, Jim Rohn, Elbert Hubbard, Aristotle, W. E. B. Du Bois, Dhirubhai Ambani, Ellen DeGeneres, Michael Jordan, Ralph Waldo Emerson, John A. Shedd, Deepak Chopra, Walter Anderson, Chinese Proverb, Lionel Messi, Tom Fleming, Maya Angelou

1. "Keep away from people who belittle your ambitions. Small people always do that, but the really great make you feel that you, too, can become great."
_____

2. "When I let go of what I am, I become what I might be."
_____

3. "Only those who will risk going too far can possibly find out how far one can go." _____

4. "Unless you choose to do great things with it, it makes no difference how much you are rewarded, or how much power you have."
_____

5. "If you do what you've always done, you'll get what you've always gotten."
_____

6. "If you're going to be thinking anything, you might as well think big."
_____

7. "Man cannot discover new oceans unless he has the courage to lose sight of the shore." _____

8. "Your time is limited, so don't waste it living someone else's life."
_____

9. "If you are not willing to risk the unusual, you will have to settle for the ordinary." _____

10. "There is only one way to avoid criticism: Do nothing, say nothing, and be nothing." _____

11. "The most important thing to remember is this: to be ready at any moment to give up what you are for what you might become."
_____

12. "If you don't build your dream, someone else will hire you to help them build theirs." _____

13. "When you take risks you learn that there will be times when you succeed and there will be times when you fail, and both are equally important."
_____

14. "I've missed more than 9000 shots in my career. I've lost almost 300 games. Twenty-six times I've been trusted to take the game-winning shot and missed. I've failed over and over and over again in my life. And that is why I succeed."
_____

15. "Don't be too timid and squeamish about your actions. All life is an experiment. The more experiments you make the better."
_____

16. "A ship in harbor is safe, but that is not what ships are built for."
_____

17. "Always go with your passions. Never ask yourself if it's realistic or not."
_____

18. "Our lives improve only when we take chances, and the first and most difficult risk we can take is to be honest with ourselves."
_____

19. "The best time to plant a tree was 20 years ago. The second best time is now." _____

20. "Twenty years from now you will be more disappointed by the things that you didn't do than by the ones you did do, so throw off the bowlines, sail away from safe harbor, catch the trade winds in your sails. Explore, dream, discover." _____

21. "I start early and I stay late, day after day, year after year, it took me 17 years and 114 days to become an overnight success." _____

22. "Somewhere in the world someone is training when you are not. When you race him, he will win." _____

23. "I've learned that people will forget what you said, people will forget what you did, but people will never forget how you made them feel."
_____

Mon	Tue	Wed	Thr	Fri	Sat	Sun	Date: _____
○	○	○	○	○	○	○	

My goal(s):

My obstacle(s):

Plan to overcome obstacle(s):

Task to overcome each obstacle:

My hopes for the future:

Visualization (I see myself there already)

It looks like
_____
It feels like
_____
I see
_____
I hear
_____
Consistant with my dreams? **Yes/No**

Resources needed:

Skills I have that will help me accomplish my goal:

Positive affirmation:

My past failures resulted from
_____

Because
_____

Lesson learned
_____

Things to remember:

I will
_____

I will not
_____

I want
_____

I don't want
_____

I am
_____

I am not
_____

Because
_____

I will reward myself:

I _____ am commiting to myself this day of _____ year _____ to do the best I can possibly do while being the best I can possibly be in order to achieve my goal. I **WILL** reach my goal by _____, after which I will reward myself with the above for a job well done.

Signature_____ Witness_____

Results:

( ) Reward claimed   Date claimed

DAY 24
Start Moving

Shake it off! You've done your best. That's good enough. You're not going to be able to please everybody. On days like this, when you're feeling a little down in the dumps, get out and do something. Call up a friend - one you haven't spoken to in a while. You'll feel much better.

At this time, you're in need of a change of scenery. You've been standing in one place too long. Start moving again. I know you're feeling a little depressed today. Down on your luck. Singing your woe is me's. You don't even know why! Don't let this bother you, my love. Use your time wisely.

When you're stuck in one place, take the opportunity to fix that one place up. Make it look good. Plan something out. Get organized. Set some goals. There's always something to do. If you can't find anything, make something up.

Little dove, get out the crayons and draw the life you want. Create something! Use this time to experiment. You never know, you may just create something useful.

Don't surround yourself with negative people. Get yourself away from that. They may be the reason you're feeling this way in the first place. You need time to recover from their negative energy. You need time to recharge. You can't do that while they're still plugged into you. You need your full energy for later on.

No, don't let them drain you. You're not an appliance. You're human. You need rest. If you follow these instructions, my friend, you'll avoid a threat of delay ahead. You're not delayed now. You're still on track. You're just looking for a plug and a tree – a plug to recharge and a tree to rest. By the end of next week, you'll be back at it again.

The debris in your path meant to stop you will help establish your new territory. You're going to be able to walk all over this. Hang in there, my love. Hang in there. Don't let issues of your past get you down. Find the humor in them. Laugh at this! Don't stress about what's already done. Fix it – if it can be fixed. Learn from it – if there's something to learn. Laugh at it, because some mistakes are funny.

Move from this, my love. Stop standing in one place. This is why you keep seeing the same thing over and over again. Move, my friend! Don't look back! You have enough charge to get to your next resting place. Once you're there, recharge and move on. Keep moving! Then keep moving! Then Keep moving.

Keep Moving Forward

Note to Self:

"As you start to walk out on the way, the way appears."

~Rumi

Journey Checklist

Create a checklist to make sure you have everything you need for *your* journey through life.

( ) _____
( ) _____
( ) _____
( ) _____
( ) _____
( ) _____
( ) _____
( ) _____
( ) _____
( ) _____
( ) _____
( ) _____
( ) _____
( ) _____
( ) _____
( ) _____
( ) _____
( ) _____
( ) _____
( ) _____
( ) _____
( ) _____
( ) _____
( ) _____
( ) _____
( ) _____
( ) _____
( ) _____
( ) _____
( ) _____

( ) _____
( ) _____
( ) _____
( ) _____
( ) _____
( ) _____
( ) _____
( ) _____
( ) _____
( ) _____
( ) _____
( ) _____
( ) _____
( ) _____
( ) _____
( ) _____
( ) _____
( ) _____
( ) _____
( ) _____
( ) _____
( ) _____
( ) _____
( ) _____
( ) _____
( ) _____
( ) _____
( ) _____
( ) _____
( ) _____
( ) _____
( ) _____
( ) _____
( ) _____
( ) _____
( ) _____
( ) _____

Mon	**Tue**	**Wed**	**Thr**	**Fri**	**Sat**	**Sun**	Date: _____
○	○	○	○	○	○	○	

My goal(s):

My obstacle(s):

Plan to overcome obstacle(s):

Task to overcome each obstacle:

My hopes for the future:

Visualization (I see myself there already)

It looks like
_____
It feels like
_____
I see
_____
I hear
_____

Consistant with my dreams? **Yes/No**

Resources needed:

Skills I have that will help me accomplish my goal:

Positive affirmation:

My past failures resulted from
_____

Because
_____

Lesson learned
_____

Things to remember:

I will
_____

I will not
_____

I want
_____

I don't want
_____

I am
_____

I am not
_____

Because
_____

I will reward myself:

I _____ am commiting to myself this day of _____ year _____ to do the best I can possibly do while being the best I can possibly be in order to achieve my goal. I **WILL** reach my goal by _____, after which I will reward myself with the above for a job well done.

Signature_____ Witness_____

Results:

( ) Reward claimed   Date claimed

DAY 25
Capable of Achieving

You're capable of achieving anything you want to achieve in life. You have the capabilities to achieve your goals. It's possible to maintain a healthy, balanced life. Envision the possibilities!

There is no one standing in your way but you! The question is: are you willing to push you down in order to be lifted up? You're not a failure until you give up. Life has more in store for you; however, you've got to be willing to keep going to get all the goodies coming your way.

It's not over! It does not matter if both the fat and the skinny lady have sung in your life. It's not over! The credits are not rolling. "They" can't give you what you need. "They" can't afford to purchase the thing coming your way. It goes above them. Yes, "they" anticipate your fall. Yes, "they" anticipate your failure, but my friend, "they" cannot stop you! Don't stop yourself.

I know it's hard trying to make ends meet right now, but suffer it to be so for the time being. There's more coming your way, my friend – unexpected abundance. You're destined to succeed! You are destined to become! You are destined to arrive! Yes, you have been set apart for a reason. There is greatness inside of you, but before you can find it, you have to find you.

It's easy to get lost in a world of lust, vanity, and greed. It's easy to be jealous of what your neighbors have – especially when they don't cease to remind you they have it. No worries, my love. Do not be in competition with them. Their success is glass in sand to your rubies.

Achieve Your Goals

Note to Self:
_____
_____
_____
_____
_____
_____
_____
_____
_____
_____

"A withered maple leaf has left its branch and is falling to the ground; its movements resemble those of a butterfly in flight. Isn't it strange? The saddest and deadest of things is yet so like the gayest and most vital of creatures?"

~Ivan Turgenev, *Fathers and Sons*

Vision Board

Plan your vision board. A vision board is like a snapshot of your dreams, goals, and things that you enjoy. It is often comprised of a collage of images, pictures, and affirmations. But it's your vision board, and on it you can put whatever you like. Use the blank space in this exercise to plan your vision board. Remember, this is just your vision board plan. Don't forget to make your vision board!

Mon	**Tue**	**Wed**	**Thr**	**Fri**	**Sat**	**Sun**	Date: _____
○	○	○	○	○	○	○	

My goal(s):

My obstacle(s):

Plan to overcome obstacle(s):

Task to overcome each obstacle:

My hopes for the future:

Visualization (I see myself there already)

It looks like
_____
It feels like
_____
I see
_____
I hear
_____
Consistant with my dreams? **Yes/No**

Resources needed:

Skills I have that will help me accomplish my goal:

31 DAYS WITH SHAN

Positive affirmation:

My past failures resulted from

_____

Because
_____
Lesson learned
_____

Things to remember:

I will
_____
I will not
_____
I want
_____
I don't want
_____
I am
_____
I am not
_____
Because
_____

I will reward myself:

I _____ am commiting to myself this day of _____ year _____ to do the best I can possibly do while being the best I can possibly be in order to achieve my goal. I **WILL** reach my goal by _____, after which I will reward myself with the above for a job well done.

Signature_____ Witness_____

Results:

( ) Reward claimed   Date claimed

DAY 26
Wishing for it All

Not all dreams are peaceful walks in gardens. Some dreams are uncomfortable. Some dreams will cause you pain and suffering. Some dreams will wake you. Some dreams will terrify you! Some dreams are not meant to be.

Some people dream big. Some people dream too small. Some people dream of things that will help them grow. Others dream of things that stunt growth. My friend, dream big, but dream with purpose.

It's not too late for your dreams to come true. I know it may look impossible, but nothing is impossible. Audrey Hepburn once said, "Nothing is impossible, the word itself says, 'I'm possible'!"

My love, you're possible! You haven't missed the opportunity. It will come again – be ready for it. There's nothing wrong with believing you can do great things. There's nothing wrong with dreaming big. Dreaming is not the problem. Your issue is what you're dreaming of. It doesn't line up with your purpose. Stop wishing it to come true! It will only set you back. It will only distract you. These things will come in due season, my love, when the soil is conditioned just right.

I'm not trying to discourage you. Keep believing you'll get healthy again. Keep believing you can start that business. Keep believing you'll fall in love and get married to a good person. Keep believing that loan will go through.

Stop believing that abusive relationship is going to get better today. Leave, my love, before it's too late. I've seen this before. I know how it's going to play out. It's not going to happen the way you're trying to make it happen. Let them go! Get your hands off this! Wake up from this nightmare, little dove. Wake up! You're resting in a negative situation. This dream is an illusion.

My love, our dreams have influence. Our dreams promote change. But our dreams have to be in line with our purpose in order to come true. Embrace clarity. Allow truth to pierce through those veils of illusion. Find your peace! Be gentle and continual. Yes. Continue to dream, but wake up from this nightmare.

Wake up to Reality

"If you're going through hell, keep going."

~Winston Churchill

Making Your Dreams Reality

There's no greater time than now to begin to live your dreams. Do you know you can make your dreams come true? Sure you can!

What are you dreaming of? *Be specific.*

_____
_____
_____
_____
_____
_____
_____
_____
_____
_____
_____
_____
_____
_____
_____
_____
_____
_____

Do you believe it's possible to make your dreams reality? **Yes/No**

What's your plan to make your dreams reality?

___

Do you believe you have what it takes? **Yes/No**

What are your goals for making your dreams reality?

There will be some bumps along the way. What's your plan to get over them?

Mon	**Tue**	**Wed**	**Thr**	**Fri**	**Sat**	**Sun**	Date: _____
○	○	○	○	○	○	○	

My goal(s):

My obstacle(s):

Plan to overcome obstacle(s):

Task to overcome each obstacle:

My hopes for the future:

Visualization (I see myself there already)

It looks like
_____

It feels like
_____

I see
_____

I hear
_____

Consistant with my dreams? **Yes/No**

Resources needed:

Skills I have that will help me accomplish my goal:

Positive affirmation:

My past failures resulted from
_____

Because
_____

Lesson learned
_____

Things to remember:

I will
_____

I will not
_____

I want
_____

I don't want
_____

I am
_____

I am not
_____

Because
_____

I will reward myself:

I _____ am commiting to myself this day of _____ year _____ to do the best I can possibly do while being the best I can possibly be in order to achieve my goal. I **WILL** reach my goal by _____, after which I will reward myself with the above for a job well done.

Signature_____ Witness_____

Results:

( ) Reward claimed   Date claimed

DAY 27
Faith vs Stupid

I am about to be very direct. What I have to say, you just might not like it. Please be warned to stop reading now. There are times you should and shouldn't make sacrifices, especially when you already have what you need. I know, "Faith is the substance of things hoped for, evidence of things not seen." However, faith is not a requirement, but using your head is.

Sometimes faith is replaced with impulse. This is stupid. Wanting something usually comes with a price, but in wanting nothing, you have everything you need. If you want more, remember there's a price for more. It's not going to come free! And it will not be cheap. The cost will be high.

You can't not pay your bills and expect things to be okay. No, they're going to cut your lights off. Pay your rent, or you'll be evicted. Pay your car note, or you'll soon be walking and begging for rides. You can't max out your credit cards and expect this debt to go away. No, it's going to impact your credit and set you back years from buying that house you've always wanted. This is not the kind of sacrifice faith requires.

The Great Spirit does not cause man to suffer. Man causes man to suffer through greed. Man causes man to suffer through hate. Man causes man to suffer from his own decisions, actions, and reactions. The evil in wicked hearts. The blind leading the blind. Good choked to death by wrong doing. Gots to be mo'e careful!

Don't be stupid. Don't let someone intimidate or manipulate you into a bad situation, especially when they'll be nowhere around to help you out. Don't do it! Your children need to eat. You have bills to pay. Keep a roof over your head.

Don't get me wrong; I'm all about faith. I wouldn't be here today if I didn't have any. It took a divine experience for me to realize that faith doesn't always work when using your head does.

I sat on that hospital bed with a smile on my face, just knowing my God was going to show up – even after Sky was already "dead." I just knew He'd breathe life back into her body. No. But this is when faith is a requirement. I kept seeing the miracle even though she was not there. Do you understand? It was a Divine working that day. Everything happened in three. I was in room 3:16. Do you understand?

My point is this. When it is God...He will let you know it's Him. Things will line up. You will feel a push or a pull, have a dream, or random strangers will approach you – just to say the same things. The Great Spirit always confirms. If it is meant to be, – it will be!

My friend, don't be stupid. Don't go jumping out an airplane without a parachute – flying high above altitude –

talking about faith. No, my friend. I am going to be frank with you. Splat! You will likely die. Don't be stupid!

No, don't leave your sure thing for man's promise of an unsure thing. Always think before you act. Don't put yourself in a bind. Don't gamble away bill money! To give your last is better than to sacrifice your last. At least then you will get it back in due season.

Take Care of Home

Note to Self:

"Be thankful for what you have; you'll end up having more.
If you concentrate on what you don't have,
you will never, ever have enough."

~Oprah Winfrey

Being Responsible

Fill in the blanks using only "Me," "Myself," and "I."

_____ will not be irresponsible. _____ will earn responsibility by proving that _____ can handle the small stuff. _____ accept responsibility for _____. _____ understand that _____ am my own responsibility. _____ will not shift blame. _____ will not make excuses. _____ will pay attention to my thoughts, choice of words, and actions.

_____ will own up to my actions and do my best to try to change the actions that have a negative effect on my life.

_____ understand excuses come in many shapes and sizes. The next time _____ find _____ in the middle of an excuse, _____ will change my words to be honest with _____. _____ will admit my mistakes and do my best to ensure _____ don't repeat them. _____ will not complain.

If _____ find _____ complaining, _____ will stop _____ to say something positive instead. _____ will not play the victim.

_____ know the world is not out to get _____. _____ will accept what _____ cannot control. _____ will surrender my will to what _____ cannot change. _____ will focus on the things that _____ can control. _____ understand _____ can't be responsible for everything.

_____ will practice self-discipline and work on developing responsible skills and habits. _____ will not blow things off or procrastinate. What _____ don't know, _____ will learn. _____ will study life's challenges and find ways to benefit from them when they happen in my life. _____ will practice positivity. _____ will plan. _____ will set goals. _____ will not allow _____ to be distracted. _____ will make a manageable to-do list every day and will try to complete as many tasks as _____ can. _____ will reward _____ for completing difficult tasks. _____ will start small when _____ I need to. _____ will do my best to stay positive, encouraged, and motivated. _____ will multitask. _____ will make sure my priorities are in order. _____ will do my best to stay financially fit by planning ahead, budgeting, doing things in moderation, and spending my money wisely. _____ will always put my needs before my wants. _____ will be reliable, persistent, and consistent. _____ will humble _____ to accept constructive criticism and feedback from others. _____ will self-access. _____ will take the initiative. _____ will care for something outside _____, and will work on developing healthy habits and routines. _____ will care for someone outside myself and will work on being helpful. _____ will be responsible.

_____ am responsible.

Mon	**Tue**	**Wed**	**Thr**	**Fri**	**Sat**	**Sun**	Date: _____
○	○	○	○	○	○	○	

My goal(s):

My obstacle(s):

Plan to overcome obstacle(s):

Task to overcome each obstacle:

My hopes for the future:

Visualization (I see myself there already)

It looks like
_____

It feels like
_____

I see
_____

I hear
_____

Consistant with my dreams? **Yes/No**

Resources needed:

Skills I have that will help me accomplish my goal:

Positive affirmation:

My past failures resulted from
_____

Because
_____

Lesson learned
_____

Things to remember:

I will
_____

I will not
_____

I want
_____

I don't want
_____

I am
_____

I am not
_____

Because
_____

I will reward myself:

I _____ am commiting to myself this day of _____ year _____ to do the best I can possibly do while being the best I can possibly be in order to achieve my goal. I **WILL** reach my goal by _____, after which I will reward myself with the above for a job well done.

Signature_____ Witness_____

Results:

( ) Reward claimed   Date claimed

DAY 28
Open the Door

The opportunity you've been waiting on isn't going to come to you. You have to go find it. It's a door – a door in a location currently out of view. You have to get on top of things to see what I see. You'll have to focus and pay attention to your surroundings. You'll have to be competent and alert. My friend, you'll have to get ready, be ready, and stay ready.

Swallow your pride. Ask for directions! It's okay to follow someone who knows the way. Besides, a great leader learns how to follow before leading. Listen. You don't know everything. They know what they're talking about. They've been there before. Once you get there, you can lead another to their opportunity. In the meantime, allow them to show you the way.

Don't go your own way. You'll just keep going in circles. Don't worry about what's behind. Keep looking forward. Your door of opportunity is not behind you; it's in front of you. On your journey, pay attention to detail. Everything is not going to be pretty. The grass is not always going to be green. The flowers are not always going to bloom. My friend, you may have to cross barren land. Things may get hectic. Don't let this discourage you. Be prepared! Keep a positive attitude about it.

Explore the boundaries. Don't neglect or use up all your resources. Don't bite the hand that feeds you. Don't curse your blessing. Don't shut the door with a bad mouth and a nasty attitude. You'll regret it later. If you follow these instructions, my love, you'll find the door of opportunity. When you find the door, don't be afraid to walk in. Open it! Destiny is waiting for you on the other side. My friend, Destiny is beautiful!

Ask for Help When It's Needed

Note to Self:
_____
_____
_____
_____
_____
_____
_____
_____

"Opportunity does not knock, it presents itself when you beat down the door."

~Kyle Chandler

Dealing with Opportunity

The door of opportunity is open. Answer the questions below before you walk in.

What is the opportunity?
What does the opportunity look like?
How will you know it's opportunity presenting itself?
What beliefs may get in the way of the opportunity?
What is the outcome you want to achieve?
Who do you know who's close to where you need to be?
Do you plan to ask them for assistance?
What weaknesses may get in the way of the opportunity?
How can your weaknesses possibly hinder you?
What strengths could assist you with the opportunity?
How specifically could your strengths help you?
How much are you willing to risk?
Are you willing to lose to gain?
What is happening in your life right now?
How can you benefit from this circumstance to help you achieve your goals?
What must you do to take advantage of this opportunity?
What are the drawbacks?
Is the outcome under your direct control?
If not, who controls it, and how can you influence them?
How much does this opportunity cost?
Can you afford to take the opportunity?
Will this opportunity hinder you?

Is it the right time and place?

How do you know it's the right time and place?

Do you have the necessary resources?

Do you have experience?

Will you get the opportunity again?

Does it feel right?

Will taking this opportunity put you at risk?

Will taking this opportunity put others at risk?

Is taking this opportunity worth it?

Note to Self:
_____
_____
_____
_____
_____
_____
_____
_____
_____
_____
_____
_____
_____
_____
_____
_____

| **Mon** | **Tue** | **Wed** | **Thr** | **Fri** | **Sat** | **Sun** | Date: _____ |
| ○ | ○ | ○ | ○ | ○ | ○ | ○ | |

My goal(s):

My obstacle(s):

Plan to overcome obstacle(s):

Task to overcome each obstacle:

My hopes for the future:

Visualization (I see myself there already)

It looks like
_____
It feels like
_____
I see
_____
I hear
_____
Consistant with my dreams? **Yes/No**

Resources needed:

Skills I have that will help me accomplish my goal:

Positive affirmation:

My past failures resulted from
_____

Because
_____

Lesson learned
_____

Things to remember:

I will
_____

I will not
_____

I want
_____

I don't want
_____

I am
_____

I am not
_____

Because
_____

I will reward myself:

I _____ am commiting to myself this day of _____ year _____ to do the best I can possibly do while being the best I can possibly be in order to achieve my goal. I **WILL** reach my goal by _____, after which I will reward myself with the above for a job well done.

Signature_____ Witness_____

Results:

( ) Reward claimed   Date claimed

DAY 29
Compassion for Others

It's not funny to laugh at the pain of another. You can laugh with them; but, not at them. Imagine that was your child. Imagine that was your mother. Imagine that was your father. Imagine that was your brother, sister, aunt, uncle, or cousin. No. It's not funny. It's rude. It's mean. It's inconsiderate. It's heartless.

You don't know their story. You don't know what they've been through. Why they're the way they are. Get off your high horse. You're not better than them. You may have a pot to piss in, but it gets dirty.

Have compassion for others. Treat people the way you would like to be treated. Would you like people to treat you less than human? Would you like people to throw things at you, or push you down? Would you like people to judge you based on color? Imagine it was you – that suffered with mental illness. No. It's not funny. It's the reason people snap. I repeat, man causes man to suffer.

My heart weeps for this world. So much hurt. So much pain! Not enough love. When will we understand? When will we understand what we're here for? We're here to become one. We are here to unite in love. We're here to assist one another on the journey. We're here to build one another up – not tare each other down. Do you understand?

You have the power to help them overcome. All you have to do is love them. In spite of it all! Love them! Love them in spite of what they look like. Love them in spite of what they smell like. Love them in spite of the way they walk. Love the in spite of the way they talk. Love them! Love them in spite of where they come from. Love them in spite of where you think they're going. Love them! If the Great Spirit cries about anything; I'm sure it would be this.

We're all God's children. We all come from the same place. There was before a beginning, and there will one day be an end. I encourage you to get it right before then.

I encourage you to fix it! I encourage you to love! I dare you to do something good for someone else today. I dare you to tell a stranger you love them. I dare you to take the shoes off your feet, and give them to someone else in need. I dare you to do something to promote love in this world. I dare you to fix it! Love them!

Mother Teresa said, "If you judge people, you have no time to love them. Kind words can be short and easy to speak, but their echoes are truly endless. If we have no peace, it is because we have forgotten that we belong to each other. Be faithful in small things because it is in them that your strength lies. If you can't feed a hundred people, then feed just one. Peace begins with a smile. Spread love everywhere you go. Let no one ever come to you without leaving happier. Every time you smile at someone, it is an action of love, a gift to that person, a beautiful thing. The hunger for love is much more difficult to remove than the hunger for bread. Do not wait for leaders; do it alone, person to person."

Love in Spite of It All

Note to Self:

"Spread love everywhere you go. Let no one ever come to you without leaving happier".

~Mother Teresa

Compassion Checklist

Check to make sure you have everything you need to be compassionate to *you*rself as well as others.

- ( ) You share
- ( ) You don't put emphasis on money
- ( ) You act on empathy
- ( ) You're kind to yourself
- ( ) You're kind to others
- ( ) You teach others
- ( ) You're mindful
- ( ) You have high emotional intelligence
- ( ) You express gratitude
- ( ) You don't judge
- ( ) You don't force your opinion
- ( ) You listen
- ( ) You volunteer
- ( ) You demonstrate acceptance
- ( ) You practice acts of kindness
- ( ) You have a routine for showing gratitude
- ( ) You're supportive
- ( ) You remember the whole person
- ( ) You communicate
- ( ) You encourage

( )   You express yourself
( )   You allow others to express themselves
( )   You respect boundaries
( )   You respect privacy
( )   You advocate
( )   You consider your words
( )   You separate the person from the behavior
( )   You're considerate
( )   You're selfless
( )   You see yourself in others
( )   You smile
( )   You're courteous
( )   You help motivate and inspire
( )   You allocate time to bond
( )   You'll choose a hug over a handshake
( )   You always say please and thank you
( )   You offer your helping hands
( )   You're truthful
( )   You make little things matter in a big way
( )   You follow the golden rule
( )   You love unconditionally
( ) _____
( ) _____
( ) _____
( ) _____
( ) _____
( ) _____

Mon	Tue	Wed	Thr	Fri	Sat	Sun	Date: _____
○	○	○	○	○	○	○	

My goal(s):

My obstacle(s):

Plan to overcome obstacle(s):

Task to overcome each obstacle:

My hopes for the future:

Visualization (I see myself there already)

It looks like
_____

It feels like
_____

I see
_____

I hear
_____

Consistant with my dreams? **Yes/No**

Resources needed:

Skills I have that will help me accomplish my goal:

Positive affirmation:

My past failures resulted from
_____

Because
_____

Lesson learned
_____

Things to remember:

I will
_____

I will not
_____

I want
_____

I don't want
_____

I am
_____

I am not
_____

Because
_____

I will reward myself:

I _____ am commiting to myself this day of _____ year _____ to do the best I can possibly do while being the best I can possibly be in order to achieve my goal. I **WILL** reach my goal by _____, after which I will reward myself with the above for a job well done.

Signature_____ Witness_____

Results:

( ) Reward claimed   Date claimed

DAY 30
Journey to Destiny

Life's a journey. It's the process to learning. You can't accomplish anything without first living. If you've ever taken a trip before, you know there's going to be some ups and downs. There's going to be some moving and shaking with the possibility of breaking. There's going to be times when a cautious halt is required. You can get lost if you don't know where you're going. You have to use a map.

I've learned on my journey that a built-in GPS is inside of me. This GPS is called spirit. Spirit is the key that helps us get going, the power and the drive that gets us there. It assures us that if we follow spirit's directions, we'll arrive – on time.

There are times when you'll lose GPS signal. What do you do? My friend, you have to keep going. You'll get it back! There are certain things we do – being human – that cause interference with spiritual communication. It's our responsibility to make sure our channels are clear. If you lose signal, don't get unnerved. Don't take a detour. Handle the unexpected with grace.

You can always call for support. Unlike roadside assistance, your Help makes house calls. He sends His employees out to hospitals, jails, shelters, bedsides, and roadsides (just to name a few). No, when something goes wrong on your journey, stay calm – it's just another lesson. Study to pass your test.

When an unexpected event causes blow out, be prepared. Use this to make that! Trust your gut. It's your GPS sending you a signal. Be patient, my love; you'll get there. It's your destiny! It only requires you to keep going.

Don't pay attention to time in this matter. Like death, it's an illusion. When stuck in traffic, go with the flow. Rushing can get you to a place called nowhere fast. Keep your eyes on the road. See things for what they are. If it looks like debris, then it's debris. If it looks like blockage, then it's blockage. If it looks like danger, then it's dangerous.

My friend, I don't know where you're going; I just know you're going somewhere. Count it all joy! It's for your good: "To give you a future and a hope." You're getting there! All you need to do is keep going. The journey to your destiny is going to be worth it.

Tune into the Inner You

"What lies behind us and what lies before us are tiny matters compared to what lies within us."

~Ralph Waldo Emerson

Write a Letter to the Inner You

Dear Self,

Mon	Tue	Wed	Thr	Fri	Sat	Sun	Date: _____
○	○	○	○	○	○	○	

My goal(s):

My obstacle(s):

Plan to overcome obstacle(s):

Task to overcome each obstacle:

My hopes for the future:

Visualization (I see myself there already)

It looks like
_____
It feels like
_____
I see
_____
I hear
_____
Consistant with my dreams? **Yes/No**

Resources needed:

Skills I have that will help me accomplish my goal:

31 DAYS WITH SHAN

Positive affirmation:

My past failures resulted from
_____

Because _____

Lesson learned _____

Things to remember:

I will _____

I will not _____

I want _____

I don't want _____

I am _____

I am not _____

Because _____

I will reward myself:

I _____ am commiting to myself this day of _____ year _____ to do the best I can possibly do while being the best I can possibly be in order to achieve my goal. I **WILL** reach my goal by _____, after which I will reward myself with the above for a job well done.

Signature_____ Witness_____

Results:

( ) Reward claimed   Date claimed

DAY 31
Be Patient

If it's worth the wait, wait for it. Beautiful, efficient things don't just happen. They go through a series of steps and/or processes. Inventions, if they're actually going to work and be successful, have to be carefully analyzed, designed, planned, interpreted, and understood before desired results are established.

Use this time to gather information. Ask questions. No, ask the right questions. My love, "Closed mouths don't get fed." Closed mouths are full of unanswered questions. Closed mouths choke to death in want – they're too afraid to ask for what they need. Ask! You never know. Ask! "Ask, and it shall be given."

Be open and honest with yourself. What are your goals? What are you looking for? What's your purpose? What's your worth? What are your wants? What are your needs? Who do you want? Who do you need? Most importantly, who are you?

Take the time to get to know everything you need to know about the subject matter, and yourself in relation to it. If not, you might miss something crucial to making this thing work. No worries. You got this!

Refrain from making decisions too early. Don't be quick to throw it away. You can fix it! You can start again! You can power up and take your life back! You can use this to make that! Give your life your best! Invent the better you! You just have to backtrack to figure out what went wrong. Remember, backtracking doesn't mean staying stuck in the past. Do a review of your life. Learn the lessons you're supposed to learn. Then work on passing your test.

Present the best you! Embrace humility! Move in action to your destiny! My friend, you will lose to gain. Let what needs to end, end so you can begin again. Don't spoil your fresh start. Free yourself! Take care of yourself! Be responsible for you! You're deserving, and you're worth it.

Now is the time to focus. Give yourself time to think about things. You don't want to rush the process. You may end up regretting it down the line. Beautiful, efficient things take time to develop. There is sure to be delay. There is sure to be an encounter with difficulty. Keep moving forward! Keep making your contribution to the world! Yes, things may not work out the way you want them to. Don't give up! Be persistent! Your dreams can become a reality in your life! You can achieve your goals! Remember to tune into the inner you and ask for help when help is needed.

My friend, if it's worth it, wait. If it's worth it, keep working at it. Love in spite of it all! My love, I think it's going to be worth the wait.

Remember to Reward Yourself

Note to Self:

"Patience serves as a protection against wrongs as clothes do against cold. For if you put on more clothes as the cold increases, it will have no power to hurt you. So in like manner you must grow in patience when you meet with great wrongs, and they will then be powerless to vex your mind."

~Leonardo da Vinci

Write a Letter to Your Future

Dear Future,

Mon	**Tue**	**Wed**	**Thr**	**Fri**	**Sat**	**Sun**	Date: _____
○	○	○	○	○	○	○	

My goal(s):

My obstacle(s):

Plan to overcome obstacle(s):

Task to overcome each obstacle:

My hopes for the future:

Visualization (I see myself there already)

It looks like
_____
It feels like
_____
I see
_____
I hear
_____

Consistant with my dreams? **Yes/No**

Resources needed:

Skills I have that will help me accomplish my goal:

Positive affirmation:

My past failures resulted from
_____

Because
_____

Lesson learned
_____

Things to remember:

I will
_____

I will not
_____

I want
_____

I don't want
_____

I am
_____

I am not
_____

Because
_____

I will reward myself:

I _____ am commiting to myself this day of _____ year _____ to do the best I can possibly do while being the best I can possibly be in order to achieve my goal. I **WILL** reach my goal by _____, after which I will reward myself with the above for a job well done.

Signature_____ Witness_____

Results:

( ) Reward claimed   Date claimed

My friend,

I realize this book can't solve your problems, but it can help you work through them. I'm proud of you for making the effort to better you. You did it! Yes. You did it! Now, keep doing it. I know it hasn't been easy. It's not easy for me either, but we have to do what we have to do to become – the world needs us.

If you have anything you'd like to share:

Write to me:
S. R. Adams, P.O. Box 2269, Oceanside, CA 92051

Email me:
Info@sradams.com

Fax Me:
1-888-512-0703

Follow Me:
Facebook - facebook.com/sradamsbrand
Twitter - twitter.com/sradamsbrand
Pinterest - pinterest.com/sradamsbrand
Instagram - instagram.com/sradamsbrand
YouTube - youtube.com/channel/UCLHmbbdZ2RWMO8-HUk5glIg
Google + - plus.google.com/112008499818207353785

Stay connected with me:
www.Sradams.com

Administer of Love
S. R. Adams

I Love You!

S. R. Adams Brand, LLC
P.O. Box 2269
Oceanside, CA 92051

Qty   SPECIAL OFFERS

_____ Hope to a Friend: Sunrise – Encouragement to Overcome
            Paperback   978-0-9977465-0-1 $10.00
_____ 31 DAYS WITH SHAN – Turning over a new leaf
            Paperback   978-0-9977465-8-7 $15.00
_____ Donation   Amount: $ _____

*Payable in U.S. funds (no cash orders accepted) – Please mail check or money orders instead. *Postage and handling: $3.00 for 1 book, 1.00 for each additional book up to a maximum of $10.00. Please allow 8 weeks for delivery.*

* Prices subject to change without notice

Subtotal $ _____
Postage and handling* $ _____
California sales tax $ _____
Total amount due $ _____

I've enclosed my: ( )Check   ( )Money Order   ( ) Card Information
Please charge my: ( )Visa   ( ) MasterCard   ( )American Express
Card# _____ Expiration date _____
Name as it appears on card _____
What is the 3-digit code found on the back of the card? _____
Address _____
City_____ State _____ Zip _____

Who's Got Mail? YOU!

Want to join my mailing list?

( ) Yes. I'd like to join your mailing list to take advantage of special offers, receive inspirational tips, get updates, and be one of the first to know about your Shananigans.

Okay. What's your email address? _____

INTOUCH™

( ) Yes. I'd like to receive motivational phone calls and text messages.

You got it! What's your phone number? _____

Premier Issue Release 2020
S. R. Adams Magazine

12 Motivating inspiring issues to help you solve your life's problems

( ) Yes. I'd like to register to receive sneak peaks, special discounts, and updates.

( ) Yes. I understand registration is FREE and that I will only be charged when I subscribe.

Okay. Just fill out the registration form below.

_____
Name   (please print)

_____
Address   Apt

_____
City/State/Zip

Dear S. R. Adams,

Stay Connected

www.SRAdams.com

Become!
111

Administer S. R. Adams

www.ingramcontent.com/pod-product-compliance
Lightning Source LLC
Chambersburg PA
CBHW022116080426
42734CB00006B/147